Microsoft®
Windows® 10
ILLUSTRATED Introductory

Microsoft®
Windows® 10
ILLUSTRATED Introductory

Barbara Clemens

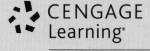
CENGAGE
Learning®

Australia • Brazil • Mexico • Singapore • United Kingdom • United States

Illustrated Microsoft® Windows® 10—Introductory
Barbara Clemens

SVP, GM Skills & Global Product Management:
    Dawn Gerrain

Product Director: Kathleen McMahon

Senior Product Team Manager: Lauren Murphy

Product Team Manager: Andrea Topping

Associate Product Manager: Reed Curry, Will Guiliani

Senior Director, Development: Marah Bellegarde

Product Development Manager: Leigh Hefferon

Senior Content Developer: Christina Kling-Garrett

Developmental Editor: MT Cozzola

Product Assistant: Erica Chapman

Marketing Director: Michele McTighe

Marketing Manager: Stephanie Albracht

Senior Production Director: Wendy Troeger

Production Director: Patty Stephan

Full Service Project Management:
    GEX Publishing Services

Designer: Diana Graham

Composition: GEX Publishing Services

Cover image(s): Lisa Kuhn, Curio Press, LLC
    www.curiopress.com

For product information and technology assistance, contact us at
Cengage Learning Customer & Sales Support, 1-800-354-9706

For permission to use material from this text or product, submit all requests online at **www.cengage.com/permissions**
Further permissions questions can be emailed to
permissionrequest@cengage.com

Library of Congress Control Number: 2015954704
ISBN-13: 978-1-305-65666-6
ISBN-10: 1-305-65666-0

Cengage Learning
20 Channel Center Street
Boston, MA 02210
USA

Cengage Learning is a leading provider of customized learning solutions with employees residing in nearly 40 different countries and sales in more than 125 countries around the world. Find your local representative at **www.cengage.com**

Cengage Learning products are represented in Canada by Nelson Education, Ltd.

For your course and learning solutions, visit **www.cengage.com**

Purchase any of our products at your local college store or at our preferred online store **www.cengagebrain.com**

Mac users: If you're working through this product using a Mac, some of the steps may vary. Additional information for Mac users is included with the Data Files for this product.

Some of the product names and company names used in this book have been used for identification purposes only and may be trademarks or registered trademarks of their respective manufacturers and sellers.

Windows® is a registered trademark of Microsoft Corporation. © 2012 Microsoft. Microsoft and the Office logo are either registered trademarks or trademarks of Microsoft Corporation in the United States and/or other countries. Cengage Learning is an independent entity from Microsoft Corporation and not affiliated with Microsoft in any manner.

Disclaimer: Any fictional data related to persons or companies or URLs used throughout this text is intended for instructional purposes only. At the time this text was published, any such data was fictional and not belonging to any real persons or companies.

Disclaimer: The material in this text was written using Microsoft Windows 10 Professional and was Quality Assurance tested before the publication date. As Microsoft continually updates the Windows 10 operating system, your software experience may vary slightly from what is presented in the printed text.

Microsoft® product screenshots used with permission from Microsoft® Corporation.

Printed in the United States of America
Print Number: 01   Print Year: 2015

Brief Contents

Contents

Getting Started with Windows 10

CASE You are about to start a new job, and your employer has asked you to get familiar with Windows 10 to help boost your productivity. You'll need to start Windows 10 and Windows apps, work with on-screen windows and commands, get help, and exit Windows. *Note: With the release of Windows 10, Microsoft now provides ongoing updates to Windows instead of releasing new versions periodically. This means that Windows features might change over time, including how they look and how you interact with them. The information provided in this text was accurate at the time this book was published.*

Module Objectives

After completing this module, you will be able to:

- Start Windows 10
- Navigate the desktop and Start menu
- Point, click, and drag
- Start an app
- Work with a window
- Manage multiple windows
- Use buttons, menus, and dialog boxes
- Get help
- Exit Windows 10

Files You Will Need

No files needed.

Start Windows 10

Learning
Outcomes
• Power on a
  computer
• Log into
  Windows 10

Windows 10 is an **operating system**, a type of program that runs your computer and lets you interact with it. A **program** is a set of instructions written for a computer. If your computer did not have an operating system, you wouldn't see anything on the screen after you turned it on. Windows 10 reserves a special area called a **Microsoft account** where each user can keep his or her files. In addition, a Microsoft account lets you use various devices and services such as a Windows Phone or Outlook.com. You may have more than one Microsoft account. When the computer and Windows 10 start, you need to **sign in**, or select your Microsoft account name and enter a password, also called **logging in**. If your computer has only one Microsoft account, you won't need to select an account name. But all users need to enter a **password**, a special sequence of numbers and letters. Users cannot see each other's account areas or services without the other person's password, so passwords help keep your computer information secure. After you sign in, you see the Windows 10 desktop, which you learn about in the next lesson. **CASE** ▶ *You're about to start a new job, so you decide to learn more about Windows 10, the operating system used at your new company.*

STEPS

1. **Press your computer's** power button, **which might look like** ⬚ **or** ⬚ , **then if the monitor is not turned on, press its** power button

   On a desktop computer, the power button is probably on the front panel. On a laptop computer it's likely at the top of the keys on your keyboard. After a few moments, a **lock screen**, showing the date, time, and an image, appears. See **FIGURE 1-1**. The lock screen appears when you first start your computer and also if you leave it unattended for a period of time.

2. **Press [Spacebar], or click once to display the sign-in screen**

   The **sign-in screen** shows your Windows account picture, name, and e-mail address, as well as a space to enter your Microsoft account password. The account may have your name assigned to it, or it might have a general name like "Student" or "Lab User."

3. **Type your** password, **as shown in** FIGURE 1-2, **using uppercase and lowercase letters as necessary**

   If necessary, ask your instructor or technical support person what password you should use. Passwords are **case sensitive**, which means that if you type any letter using capital letters when lowercase letters are needed, or vice versa, Windows will not let you use your account. For example, if your password is "booklet43+", typing "Booklet43+" or "BOOKLET43+" will not let you enter your account. For security, Windows substitutes bullets for the password characters you type.

4. **Click or tap the** Submit button ⬚

   The Windows 10 desktop appears. See **FIGURE 1-3**.

Using a touch screen with Windows

Windows 10 was developed to work with touch-screen computers, including tablets and smartphones. See **FIGURE 1-4**. So if you have a touch-screen device, you'll find that you can accomplish many tasks with gestures instead of a mouse. A **gesture** is an action you take with your fingertip directly on the screen, such as tapping or swiping. For example, when you sign into Windows 10, you can tap the Submit button on the screen, instead of clicking it.

FIGURE 1-4: Touch-screen device

© vovan/Shutterstock.com

FIGURE 1-1: Lock screen with time and date

Your lock screen contents may differ →

FIGURE 1-2: Typing your password

FIGURE 1-3: Windows 10 desktop

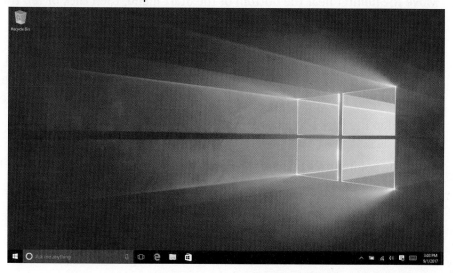

Navigate the Desktop and Start Menu

Learning Outcomes
- Examine the desktop
- Open the Start menu
- View Start menu apps
- Close the Start menu

Every time you start your computer and sign in, the Windows 10 desktop appears. The **Windows 10 desktop** is an electronic work area that lets you organize and manage your information, much like your own physical desktop. The desktop contains controls that let you interact with the Windows 10 operating system. These controls are called its **user interface (UI)**. The Windows 10 user interface is called the **Windows 10 UI.** **CASE** ➤ *To become better acquainted with Windows 10, you decide to explore the desktop and Start menu.*

STEPS

TROUBLE

If you don't see the taskbar at the bottom of the screen, it may be set to automatically hide. Move the mouse pointer to the bottom edge of the screen to display it; on a touch screen, swipe up from the bottom of the screen.

1. **Examine the Windows 10 desktop**

   As shown in **FIGURE 1-5**, the desktop currently contains one item, an icon representing the **Recycle Bin**, an electronic wastepaper basket. You might see other icons, files, and folders placed there by previous users or by your school lab. The desktop lets you manage the files and folders on your computer. A **file** is a collection of stored information, such as a letter, video, or program. A **folder** is a container that helps you organize your files. A file, folder, or program opens in a window. You can open multiple windows on the desktop at once, and you can move them around so you can easily go back and forth between them. You work with windows later in this module. At the bottom of the screen is a bar called the **taskbar**, with buttons representing commonly used programs and tools. In a default Windows installation, the taskbar contains four buttons, described in **TABLE 1-1**. Also on the taskbar is the search box, which you can use to find an item on your computer or the Internet. On the right side of the status bar you see the **Notification area**, containing the time and date as well as icons that tell you the status of your computer. At the left side of the taskbar, you see the Start button. You click the **Start button** to display the **Start menu**, which lets you start the programs on your computer.

QUICK TIP

To add a button to the taskbar, right-click or tap and hold a Start menu item, then click or tap Pin to taskbar.

2. **Move the pointer to the left side of the taskbar, then click or tap the** Start button ⊞

   The Start menu appears, as shown in **FIGURE 1-6**. Your user account name and an optional picture appear at the top. The menu shows a list of often-used programs and other controls on the left, and variously-sized shaded rectangles called **tiles** on the right. Each tile represents an **app**, short for **application program**. Some tiles show updated content using a feature called **live tile**; for example, the Weather app can show the current weather for any city you choose. (Your screen color and tiles may differ from the figures shown here. Note that the screens in this book do not show live tiles.)

QUICK TIP

You can also click or tap any category letter to display a grid of clickable or tappable letters. Or just begin typing any program name, and it appears at the top of a list of choices.

3. **Move the pointer near the bottom of the Start menu, then click or tap the** All apps **button**

   You see an alphabetical listing of all the apps on your computer. Only some of the apps are visible.

4. **Move the pointer into the list, until the gray scroll bar appears on the right side of the list, place the pointer over the** scroll box, **press and hold down the** mouse button, **then drag to display the remaining programs; on a touch screen, swipe the list to scroll**

5. **Click or tap the** Back button **at the bottom of the Start menu**

   The previous listing reappears.

QUICK TIP

You can quickly open and close the Start menu by pressing ⊞ on your keyboard.

6. **Move the pointer back up over the desktop, then click or tap once to close the Start menu**

FIGURE 1-5: Windows 10 desktop

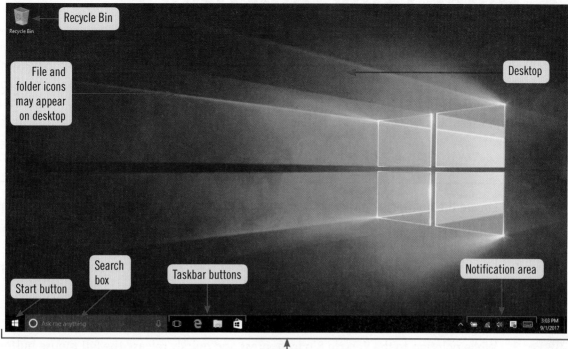

FIGURE 1-6: Start menu

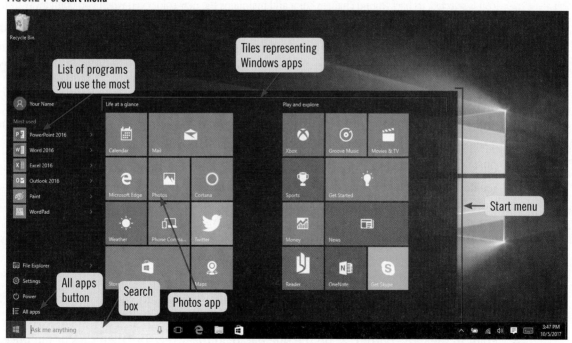

TABLE 1-1: Windows taskbar buttons

button	looks like	what it does
Task View		Shows miniatures of all open windows and lets you create multiple desktops, so you can switch from one to another
Microsoft Edge		Opens the Microsoft Edge web browser
File Explorer		Lets you explore the files in your storage locations
Store		Opens the Windows Store featuring downloadable apps, games, music, movies, and TV

Point, Click, and Drag

Learning
Outcomes
• Point to, select,
  and deselect a
  desktop icon
• Move a desktop
  icon

You communicate with Windows 10 using a variety of pointing devices (or, with a touch-screen device, your finger). A **pointing device** controls the movement of the **pointer**, a small arrow or other symbol that moves on the screen. Your pointing device could be a mouse, trackball, graphics tablet, or touchpad. There are five basic **pointing device actions** you use to communicate with your computer; see TABLE 1-2. Touch-screen users can tap, press, and tap and hold. **CASE** *You practice the basic pointing device actions.*

STEPS

QUICK TIP
A pointing device
might be attached to
your computer with
a cable, connected
wirelessly, or built
into your computer.

1. **Locate the pointer ⇱ on the desktop, then move your pointing device left, right, up, and down (or move your finger across a touch pad or screen)**
   The pointer shape ⇱ is the **Select pointer**. The pointer moves in the same direction as your device.

2. **Move your pointing device so the Select pointer is over the Recycle Bin (if you are using a touch screen, skip this step)**
   You are **pointing to** the Recycle Bin icon. The icon becomes **highlighted**, looking as though it is framed in a box with a lighter color background. (Note that touch-screen users cannot point to items.)

QUICK TIP
If you are using a
pointing device, the
pointer's shape
changes depending
on both where you
point and the
options available to
you when you point.

3. **While pointing to the Recycle Bin icon, press and quickly release the left mouse button once (or tap the icon once), then move the pointer away from the Recycle Bin icon**
   You click or tap a desktop icon once to **select** it, which signals that you intend to perform an action. When an icon is selected, its background changes color and maintains the new color even when you point away from it.

4. **With a pointing device, point to (don't click) the Microsoft Edge button 🅔 on the taskbar**
   The button becomes highlighted and an informational message called a **ScreenTip** identifies the program the button represents. ScreenTips are useful because they help you to learn about the tools available to you. **Microsoft Edge** is the new Microsoft web browser that lets you display and interact with webpages.

5. **If you are using a pointing device, move the pointer over the time and date in the notification area on the right side of the taskbar, read the ScreenTip, then click or tap once**
   A pop-up window appears, containing the current time and date and a calendar.

TROUBLE
If a window didn't
open, try again with a
faster double-click.

6. **Click or tap on the desktop, point to the Recycle Bin icon, then quickly click or tap twice**
   You **double-clicked** (or double-tapped) the icon. You need to double-click or double-tap quickly, without moving the pointer. A window opens, showing the contents of the Recycle Bin, as shown in **FIGURE 1-7**. The area at the top of the window is the title bar, which displays the name of the window. The area below the title bar is the **Ribbon**, which contains tabs, commands, and the Address bar. **Tabs** are groupings of **buttons** and other controls you use to interact with an object or a program.

7. **Click or tap the View tab**
   The buttons on that tab appear. Buttons act as **commands**, which instruct Windows to perform tasks. The **Address bar** shows the name and location of the item you have opened.

8. **Point to the Close button ☒ on the title bar, read the ScreenTip, then click or tap once**

QUICK TIP
You use dragging to
move folders, files,
and other objects on
the desktop.

9. **Point to the Recycle Bin icon, hold down the left mouse button, or press and hold the Recycle Bin image with your finger, move the mouse or drag so the object moves right as shown in FIGURE 1-8, release the mouse button or lift your finger, then drag the Recycle Bin back to its original location**

FIGURE 1-7: Recycle Bin window

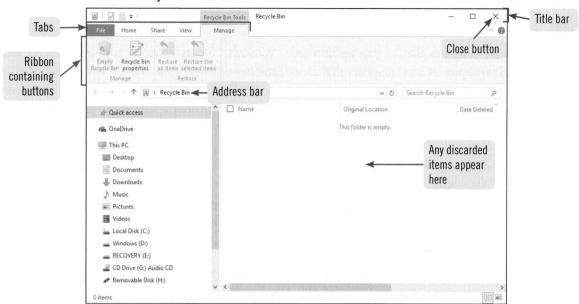

Tabs

Ribbon
containing
buttons

Address bar

Title bar

Close button

Any discarded
items appear
here

FIGURE 1-8: Dragging the Recycle Bin icon

Releasing mouse
button moves object
to this location

TABLE 1-2: Basic pointing device actions

action	with a mouse	with a touch pad	use to
Point	Move mouse to position tip of pointer over an item	Move your finger over touch pad to position tip of pointer over an item	Highlight items or display small informational boxes called ScreenTips
Click	Press and release left mouse button once	Tap touch pad once	Select objects or commands, open menus or items on the taskbar
Double-click	Quickly press and release left mouse button twice	Tap touch pad twice in quick succession	Open programs, folders, or files represented by desktop icons
Drag	Point to an object, press and hold down left mouse button, move object to a new location, then release mouse button	Slide finger across touch pad to point to an object, press and hold left touch pad button, drag across touch pad to move object to new location, then release button	Move objects, such as icons, on the desktop
Right-click	Point to an object, then press and release right mouse button	Point to an object, then press and release right touchpad button	Display a shortcut menu containing options specific to the object

Selecting and moving items using touch-screen devices

If you use a touch-screen computer, a tablet, or a smartphone, you click desktop items by tapping them once on the screen. Tap an icon twice quickly to double-click and open its window. Press and hold an icon, then drag to move it. A touch-screen device does not let you point to an object without selecting it, however, as mice and touchpads do.

Start an App

**Learning
Outcomes**
• Open the Start
  menu
• Start a Windows
  app
• Start a desktop app
• Close an app

Apps are programs that let you perform tasks. Windows 10 runs Windows apps and desktop apps. **Windows apps** are small programs that are available free or for purchase in the Windows Store, and can run on Windows desktops, laptops, tablets, and phones. Windows apps are also called **universal apps**. They are specially designed so they can stay open as you work without slowing down your computer, and often have a single purpose. Examples include the Photos app, which lets you view your photographs, and the OneDrive app, which lets you connect to files and programs you have stored on the Microsoft OneDrive website. **Desktop apps** are fully-featured programs; they may be available at an online store or on disk. For example, Microsoft Word allows you to create and edit letters, reports, and other text-based documents. Some smaller desktop apps called **Windows accessories**, such as Paint and Notepad, come already installed in Windows 10. **CASE** ▸ *To prepare for your new job, you start three apps.*

STEPS

1. **Click or tap the Start button ⊞, then click or tap the Weather tile, shown in FIGURE 1-9**
   The Weather app opens, letting you find the current weather in various locations.

2. **If you are asked to choose a location, begin typing your city or town, then click the full name if it appears in the drop-down list**
   The current weather for your selected city appears in Summary view. **FIGURE 1-10** shows a forecast for Boston, MA.

QUICK TIP
If you have Microsoft
Office installed on
your computer, you
might also see the
OneNote 2016
desktop app, as
shown in the figure.

3. **Click or tap the Weather app window's Close button ✕**

4. **Click or tap ⊞, then type onenote**
   Typing an app name is another way to locate an app. At the top of the Start menu, you see the OneNote Trusted Windows Store app listed, as shown in **FIGURE 1-11**. OneNote is a popular app that lets you create tabbed notebooks where you can store text, images, files, and media such as audio and video.

QUICK TIP
Some programs have
both full-featured
desktop apps and
reduced, often free,
Windows apps.

5. **Click or tap the OneNote Trusted Windows Store app name**
   The OneNote app opens, showing a blank notebook (or a notebook you have previously created).

6. **Click or tap the Close button ✕ in the upper right corner of the OneNote app window**
   You have opened two Windows apps, Weather and OneNote.

7. **Click or tap ⊞, then type paint**
   The top of the Start menu lists the Paint Desktop app, shown in **FIGURE 1-12**. Paint is a simple accessory that comes installed with Windows and lets you create simple illustrations.

QUICK TIP
You can also start a
desktop app by
clicking or tapping All
apps, then clicking or
tapping the app
name in the scrollable
list on the left side of
the Start menu.

8. **Click or tap the Paint Desktop app name at the top of the Start menu**
   Other accessories besides Paint and Notepad include the Snipping Tool, which lets you capture an image of any screen area, and Sticky Notes, that let you create short notes.

Using the Windows Store

The Windows Store is an app that lets you find all kinds of apps for use on Windows personal computers, tablets, and phones. You can open it by clicking or tapping its tile on the Start menu or by clicking or tapping the Store button on the taskbar. To use the Windows Store, you need to be signed in to your Microsoft account. You can browse lists of popular apps, games, music, movies, and TV including new releases; you can browse the top

paid or free apps. Browse app categories to find a specific type of app, such as Business or Entertainment. To locate a specific app, type its name in the Search box. If an app is free, you can go to its page and click the Free button to install it on your computer. If it's a paid app, you can click or tap the Free trial button to try it out, or click or tap its price button to purchase it. Any apps you've added recently appear in the Recently added category of the Start menu.

FIGURE 1-9: Weather tile on the Start menu

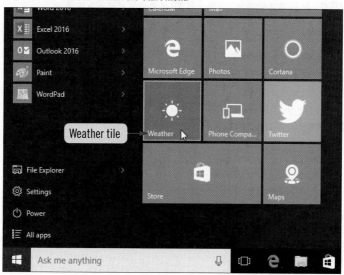

FIGURE 1-10: Weather app

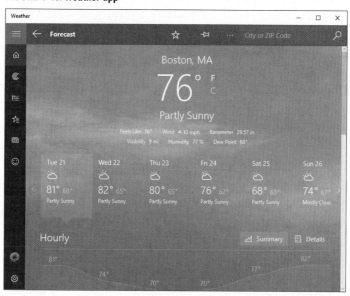

FIGURE 1-11: OneNote Windows app name on Start menu

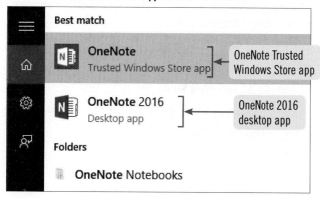

FIGURE 1-12: Paint Desktop app name on Start menu

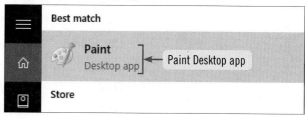

Work with a Window

Learning Outcomes
- Minimize, restore, and maximize a window
- Scroll a window
- Move a window

When you start an app, its **window**, a frame displaying the app's tools, opens. In many apps, a blank file also opens so you can start creating a new document. For example, in Paint, a blank document opens so you can start drawing right away. All windows in the Windows 10 operating system have similar window elements. Once you can use a window in one app, you will know how to work with windows in many other apps. **CASE** *To become more familiar with the Windows 10 user interface, you explore elements in the Paint window.*

DETAILS

Many windows have the following common elements. Refer to FIGURE 1-13:

- At the top of the window, you see a **title bar**, a strip that contains the name of the document and app. This document has not been saved, so it has the temporary name "Untitled" and the app name is "Paint."

- On the right side of the title bar, the **Window control buttons** let you control the app window. The **Minimize button** ☐ temporarily hides the window, making it a button on the taskbar. The app is still running, but its window is temporarily hidden until you click its taskbar button or its miniature window in Task view to reopen it. The **Maximize button** ☐ enlarges the window to fill the entire screen. If a window is already maximized, the Maximize button changes to the **Restore Down button** ☐, which reduces it to the last non-maximized size. Clicking or tapping the **Close button** ☒ closes the app.

- Many windows have a **scroll bar** on the right side and/or the bottom of the window. You click (or press) and drag scroll bar elements to show additional parts of your document. See **TABLE 1-3**.

- Just below the title bar is the Ribbon, a bar containing tabs as well as a Help icon. The Paint window has three tabs: File, Home, and View. Tabs are divided into **groups** of buttons and tool palettes. The Home tab has five groups: Clipboard, Image, Tools, Shapes, and Colors. Many apps also include **menus** you click to show lists of commands, as well as **toolbars** containing buttons.

- The **Quick Access toolbar** lets you quickly perform common actions such as saving a file.

STEPS

1. **Click or tap the Paint window** Minimize button ☐
   The app is reduced to a taskbar button, as shown in **FIGURE 1-14**. The contrasting line indicates the app is still open.

2. **Click or tap the taskbar button representing the** Paint app 🎨 **to redisplay the app**

3. **Drag the gray** scroll box **down, notice the lower edge of the work area that appears, then click or tap the** Up scroll arrow ⏶ **until you see the top edge of the work area**

4. **Point to the** View tab, **then click or tap the** View tab **once**
   Clicking or tapping the View tab moved it in front of the Home tab. This tab has three groups containing buttons that let you change your view of the document window.

5. **Click the** Home tab, **then click or tap the Paint window** Maximize button ☐
   The window fills the screen, and the Maximize button becomes the Restore Down button ☐.

6. **Click the window's** Restore Down button ☐ **to return it to its previous size**

7. **Point to the** Paint window title bar **(if you are using a pointing device), then drag about an inch to the right to move it so it's centered on the screen**

FIGURE 1-13: Typical app window elements

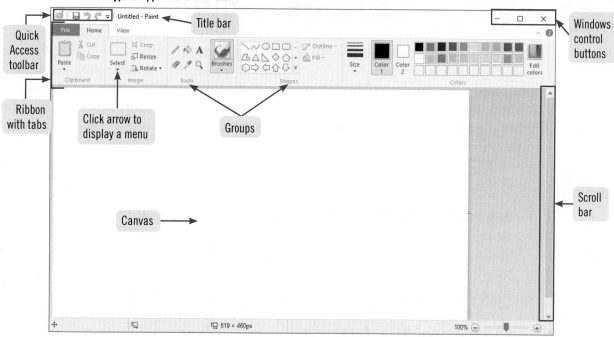

Quick Access toolbar

Title bar

Windows control buttons

Ribbon with tabs

Click arrow to display a menu

Groups

Scroll bar

Canvas

FIGURE 1-14: Taskbar with minimized Paint program button

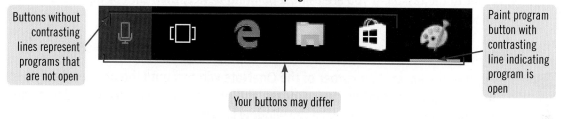

Buttons without contrasting lines represent programs that are not open

Paint program button with contrasting line indicating program is open

Your buttons may differ

TABLE 1-3: Parts of a scroll bar

name	looks like	to use
Scroll box	☐ (Size may vary)	Drag to scroll quickly through a long document
Scroll arrows	∧ ∨	Click or tap to scroll up, down, left, or right in small amounts
Shaded area	(Above, below, or to either side of scroll box)	Click or tap to move up or down by one screen

Using the Quick Access toolbar

On the left side of the title bar, the Quick Access toolbar lets you perform common tasks with just one click. The Save button 💾 saves the changes you have made to a document. The Undo button 🔄 lets you reverse (undo) the last action you performed.

The Redo button ↻ reinstates the change you just undid. Use the Customize Quick Access Toolbar button ⏷ to add other frequently used buttons to the toolbar, move the toolbar below the Ribbon, or minimize the Ribbon to show only tabs.

Manage Multiple Windows

Learning Outcomes
- Open a second app
- Activate a window
- Resize, snap, and close a window

You can work with more than one app at a time by switching among open app windows. If you open two or more apps, a window opens for each one. You can work with app windows individually, going back and forth between them. The window in front is called the **active window**. Any open window behind the active window is called an **inactive window**. For ease in working with multiple windows, you can move, arrange, make them smaller or larger, minimize, or restore them so they're not in the way. To resize a window, drag a window's edge, called its **border**. You can use the taskbar to switch between windows. See **TABLE 1-4** for a summary of taskbar actions. **CASE** *Keeping the Paint app open, you open the OneNote app and then work with both app windows.*

STEPS

1. **With Paint open, click or tap the Start button ⊞, then the OneNote tile**

   The OneNote window appears as a second window on the desktop, as shown in **FIGURE 1-15**. The OneNote window is in front, indicating that it is the active window. The Paint window is the inactive window. On the taskbar, the contrasting line under the OneNote and Paint app buttons tell you both apps are open.

2. **Point to a blank part of the OneNote window title bar on either side of the app name (if you are using a pointing device), then drag the OneNote window down slightly so you can see more of the Paint window**

3. **Click or tap once on the Paint window's title bar**

   The Paint window is now the active window and appears in front of the OneNote window. You can make any window active by clicking or tapping it, or by clicking or tapping an app's icon in the taskbar.

4. **Point to the taskbar if you are using a pointing device, then click or tap the OneNote window button**

   The OneNote window becomes active. When you open multiple windows on the desktop, you may need to resize windows so they don't get in the way of other open windows.

5. **Point to the lower-right corner of the OneNote window until the pointer changes to ⬦, if you are using a pointing device, or tap and press the corner, then drag down and to the right about an inch to make the window larger**

   You can also point to any edge of a window until you see the ⬌ or ⬍ pointer, or tap and press any edge, then drag to make it larger or smaller in one direction only.

6. **Click or tap the Task View button ▣ on the taskbar, click or tap the Paint window, click or tap ▣ again, then click or tap the OneNote window**

   The **Task View button** is another convenient way to switch among open windows.

7. **Point to the OneNote window title bar if you are using a pointing device, drag the window to the left side of the screen until the pointer or your finger reaches the screen edge and you see a vertical line down the middle of the screen, then release the mouse button or lift your finger from the screen**

   The OneNote window instantly fills the left side of the screen, and any inactive windows appear on the right side of the screen. This is called the **Snap Assist** feature. You can also drag to any screen corner to snap open app windows to quarter-screen windows.

8. **Click or tap anywhere on the reduced-size version of the Paint window**

   The Paint window fills the right side of the screen. Snapping makes it easy to view the contents of two windows at the same time. See **FIGURE 1-16**.

9. **Click or tap the OneNote window Close button ✖, then click or tap the Maximize button ▢ in the Paint window's title bar**

   The OneNote app closes. The Paint app window remains open.

FIGURE 1-15: Working with multiple windows

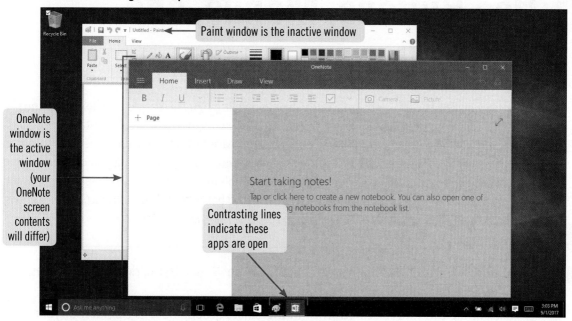

Paint window is the inactive window

OneNote window is the active window (your OneNote screen contents will differ)

Contrasting lines indicate these apps are open

FIGURE 1-16: OneNote and Paint windows snapped to each side of the screen

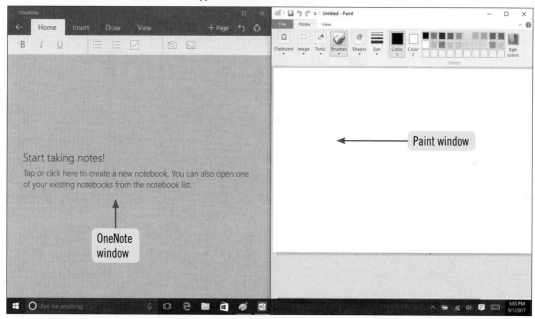

Paint window

OneNote window

TABLE 1-4: Using the taskbar

to	do this
Add buttons to taskbar	Open an app, right-click or press its icon on the taskbar, then click or tap Pin this program to taskbar
Change order of taskbar buttons	Drag any icon to a new taskbar location
See a list of recent documents opened	Right-click or press taskbar app button
Close a document using the taskbar	Point to taskbar button, point to document image, then click its Close button
Minimize/Redisplay all open windows	Click or press Show desktop button (the thin bar) to the right of taskbar date and time
See preview of documents in taskbar	With a pointing device, point to taskbar button for open app
Bring a minimized window to the front	Click or press the Task View button, then click or tap the window or desktop you want in front
Rearrange windows on the desktop	Right-click taskbar, click Cascade Windows, Show windows stacked, or Show windows side by side

Use Buttons, Menus, and Dialog Boxes

Learning Outcomes
- Use a button and a menu
- Work in a dialog box

When you work in an app, you communicate with it using buttons, menus, and dialog boxes. **Buttons** let you issue instructions to modify app objects. Buttons are often organized on a Ribbon into tabs, and then into groups like those in the Paint window. Some buttons have text on them, and others show only an icon that represents what they do. Other buttons reveal **menus**, lists of commands you can choose. And some buttons open up a **dialog box**, a window with controls that lets you tell Windows what you want. **TABLE 1-5** lists the common types of controls you find in dialog boxes. **CASE** *You practice using buttons, menus, and dialog boxes to create some simple graphics in the Paint app.*

STEPS

1. **In the Shapes group, click or tap the** More button ▼ **just to the right of the shapes, then click the** Triangle button △

2. **Click or tap the** Turquoise button ▨ **in the Colors group, move the pointer or your finger over the white drawing area, then drag down and to the right, to draw a** triangle **similar to the one in FIGURE 1-17**
   The white drawing area is called the **canvas**.

3. **In the Shapes group, click or tap** ▼, **click the** down scroll arrow if necessary, **click or tap the** Five-point star button, **click or tap the** Indigo color button ▨ **in the Colors group, then drag a star shape near the triangle, using FIGURE 1-17 as a guide**
   Don't be concerned if your object isn't exactly like the one in the figure, or in exactly the same place.

4. **Click or tap the** Fill with color button ▨ **in the Tools group, click or tap the** Light turquoise color button ▨ **in the Colors group, click or tap inside the** triangle, **click or tap the** Purple color button ▨, **click or tap inside the** star, **then compare your drawing to FIGURE 1-17**

5. **Click or tap the** Select list arrow **in the Image group, then click or tap** Select all, **as shown in FIGURE 1-18**
   The Select all command selects the entire drawing, as indicated by the dotted line surrounding the white drawing area. Other commands on this menu let you select individual elements or change your selection.

6. **Click or tap the** Rotate button **in the Image group, then click or tap** Rotate 180°
   You often need to use multiple commands to perform an action—in this case, you used one command to select the items you wanted to work with, and another command to rotate them.

7. **Click or tap the** File tab, **then click or tap** Print
   The Print dialog box opens, as shown in **FIGURE 1-19**. This dialog box lets you choose a printer, specify which part of your document or drawing you want to print, and choose how many copies you want to print. The **default**, or automatically selected, number of copies is 1, which is what you want.

8. **Click or tap** Print, **or if you prefer not to print, click or tap** Cancel
   The drawing prints on your printer. You decide to close the app without saving your drawing.

9. **Click or tap the** File tab, **click or tap** Exit, **then click or tap** Don't Save
   You closed the file without saving your changes, then exited the app. Most apps include a command for closing a document without exiting the program. However, Paint allows you to open only one document at a time, so it does not include a Close command.

FIGURE 1-17: Triangle and star shapes filled with color

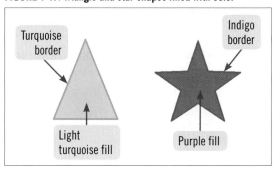

Turquoise border

Indigo border

Light turquoise fill

Purple fill

FIGURE 1-18: Select menu options

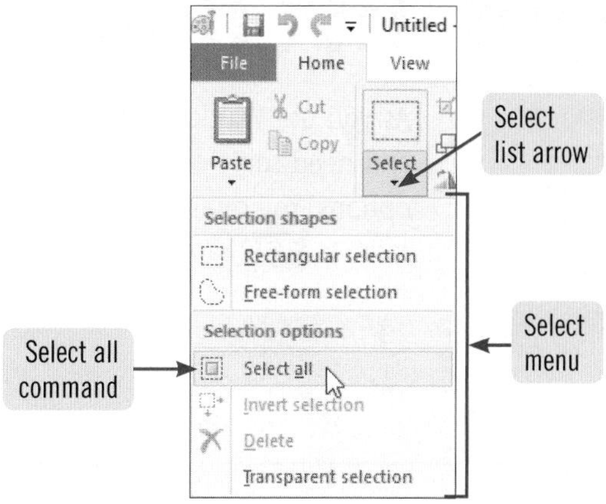

Select list arrow

Select menu

Select all command

FIGURE 1-19: Print dialog box

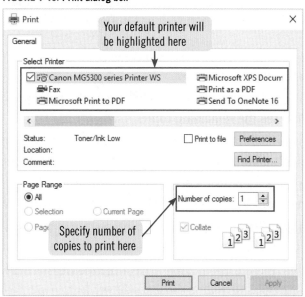

Your default printer will be highlighted here

Specify number of copies to print here

TABLE 1-5: Common dialog box controls

element	example	description
Text box	1 - 27	A box in which you type text or numbers
Spin box	1	A box with up and down arrows; you can click or tap arrows or type to increase or decrease value
Option button		A small circle you click or tap to select the option; only one in a set can be selected at once
Check box		A small box that turns an option on when checked or off when unchecked; more than one in a set can be selected at once
List box		A box that lets you select from a list of options
Button	Save	A button you click or tap to issue a command

Get Help

As you use Windows 10, you might feel ready to learn more about it, or you might have a problem and need some advice. You can use the Windows 10 Getting Started app to learn more about help options. You can also search for help using Cortana, which you activate by using the search box on the taskbar. **CASE** *You explore Windows 10 help using the Get Started app and Cortana.*

STEPS

Note: Because Help in an online resource, topics and information are liable to change over time. If your screen choices do not match the steps below exactly, be flexible by exploring the options that are available to you and searching for the information you need.

1. Click or tap the Start button ⊞, then in the Explore Windows section click or tap the Get Started tile; if the Explore Windows section does not appear on your Start menu, begin typing Get Started, then click or tap Get Started Trusted Windows Store app in the list

   The Get Started app window opens. The window contains a menu expand button ☰ in the upper left and a bar containing buttons on the left side.

2. Click or tap the Menu Expand button ☰, move the pointer over the list of topics, then scroll down to see the remaining topics

3. Click or tap the Search and help topic, click the Search for anything, anywhere tile, then read the information, as shown in FIGURE 1-20, scrolling as necessary

4. Click or tap the Back button ← in the top-left corner of the window, click the Search for help tile, then read the Search for help topic and watch any available videos

5. Click or tap ☰, click or tap a topic that interests you, then read the information or click or tap one of the tiles representing a subtopic if one is available

6. After you have read the information, click or tap the Get started window's Close button ✕

   As the Help topic explained, you can also search the web for help with Windows using Cortana.

7. Click in the search box on the taskbar, then type windows help

   As you type, Cortana begins a search, and shows results on the Start menu. See FIGURE 1-21. Your results may also include topics from the Microsoft Store, the web, Store apps, and OneDrive, your online storage location.

8. Click any web option that interests you

9. When you are finished, click or tap the window's Close button ✕ to return to the desktop

FIGURE 1-20: Get Started Search and Help topic

Menu Expand button

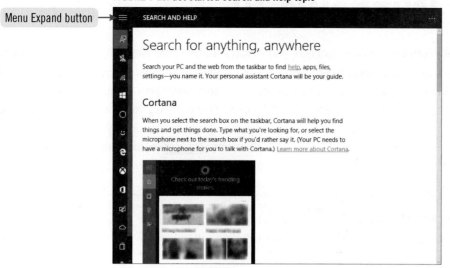

FIGURE 1-21: Search results information

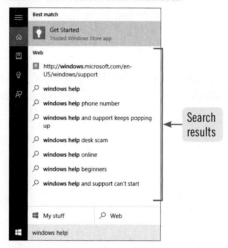

Search results

Using Cortana

Cortana is the digital personal assistant that comes with Windows 10 and Windows phones. You can interact with Cortana typing or using your voice. Use Cortana to search the web, remind you of events or appointments, set alarms, change computer settings, get directions, get current news and weather, track airline flights, play, and even identify music. **FIGURE 1-22** shows Cortana's response to "What's the weather in New York?" which may also give a voice response. You call Cortana by saying, "Hey Cortana," or by clicking or tapping the microphone icon on the right side of the taskbar search box, and then asking a question or saying a command. Depending on your request, Cortana may reply out loud, display results in the Start menu, or display results in a Microsoft Edge web browser window. You may need to set up Cortana on your computer and answer security questions before you use it. The first time you use Cortana, you may be asked to answer questions to help the assistant recognize your voice or solve issues with your computer's microphone.

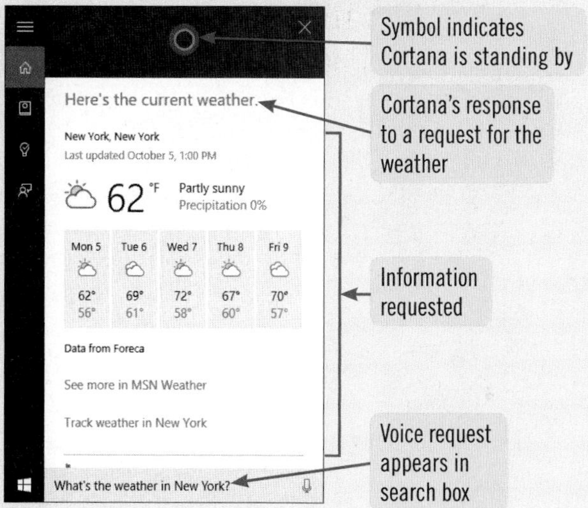

FIGURE 1-22: Using Cortana to check the weather

Symbol indicates Cortana is standing by

Cortana's response to a request for the weather

Information requested

Voice request appears in search box

Exit Windows 10

**Learning
Outcomes**
• Exit Windows and
shut down

When you finish working on your computer, you should close any open files, exit any open apps, close any open windows, and exit (or **shut down**) Windows 10. TABLE 1-6 shows options for ending your Windows 10 sessions. Whichever option you choose, it's important to shut down your computer in an orderly way. If you turn off or unplug the computer while Windows 10 is running, you could lose data or damage Windows 10 and your computer. If you are working in a computer lab, follow your instructor's directions and your lab's policies for ending your Windows 10 session. **CASE** *You have examined the basic ways you can use Windows 10, so you are ready to end your Windows 10 session.*

STEPS

QUICK TIP
Instead of shutting down, you may be instructed to sign out, or log out, of your Microsoft account. Click or tap Start, click or tap your account name, then click or tap Sign out.

1. **Click or tap the** Start button ⊞**, then click or tap** Power
   The Power button menu lists shut down options, as shown in **FIGURE 1-23**.

2. **If you are working in a computer lab, follow the instructions provided by your instructor or technical support person for ending your Windows 10 session; if you are working on your own computer, click or tap** Shut down **or the option you prefer for ending your Windows 10 session**

QUICK TIP
If you are using a Windows 10 tablet, press the lock button on your tablet to bring up the lock screen, swipe the lock screen, then click or tap the Shut down button to power off your computer.

3. **After you shut down your computer, you may also need to turn off your monitor and other hardware devices, such as a printer, to conserve energy**

FIGURE 1-23: Shutting down your computer

Shutdown options

Power button

TABLE 1-6: Power options

option	description
Sleep	Puts computer in a low-power state while keeping any open apps open so you can return immediately to where you left off
Shut down	Closes any open apps and completely turns off the computer
Restart	Closes any open apps, shuts down the computer, then restarts it

Installing updates when you exit Windows

Sometimes, after you shut down your machine, you might find that your machine does not shut down immediately. Instead, Windows might install software updates. If you see an option on your Power menu that lets you update, you can click or tap it to update your software. If you see a window indicating that updates are being installed, do not unplug or press the power switch to turn off your machine. Let the updates install completely. After the updates are installed, your computer will shut down, as you originally requested.

Practice

Concepts Review

Label the elements of the Windows 10 window shown in FIGURE 1-24.

FIGURE 1-24

Match each term with the statement that best describes it.

9. **Cortana**
10. **Snap Assist**
11. **Desktop app**
12. **Microsoft account**
13. **User interface**
14. **Operating system**
15. **Windows app**

a. A special area of the operating system where your files and settings are stored
b. Controls that let you interact with an operating system
c. The personal digital assistant in Windows 10
d. Full-featured program that is installed on a personal computer
e. Feature that displays windows at full height next to each other on the screen
f. Available from the Windows store, it runs on Windows laptops, tablets, and phones
g. A program necessary to run your computer

Select the best answer from the list of choices.

16. **The bar containing buttons and other elements at the bottom of the Windows 10 desktop is called the _____.**

   a. title bar
   b. address bar
   c. scroll bar
   d. taskbar

17. **Paint is an example of a(n) _____.**

   a. group
   b. accessory
   c. active window
   d. operating system

18. **Which of the following is in the upper-left corner of a program window, and lets you perform common actions?**
   a. Application program
   b. Quick Access toolbar
   c. Operating system
   d. Accessory program

19. **The new Microsoft web browser is called Microsoft _____.**
   a. Paint
   b. WordPad
   c. Edge
   d. File Explorer

Skills Review

1. **Start Windows 10.**
   a. If your computer and monitor are not running, press your computer's and (if necessary) your monitor's power buttons.
   b. If necessary, select the user name that represents your user account.
   c. Enter your password, using correct uppercase and lowercase letters.

2. **Navigate the desktop and Start menu.**
   a. Examine the Windows 10 desktop.
   b. Open the Start menu.
   c. Display all the apps using a command on the Start menu, and scroll the list.
   d. Return to the Start menu.
   e. Close the Start menu.

3. **Point, click, and drag.**
   a. On the Windows 10 desktop, click or tap to select the Recycle Bin.
   b. Point to display the ScreenTip for Microsoft Edge in the taskbar, and then display the ScreenTip for each of the other icons on the taskbar.
   c. Double-click or double-tap to open the Recycle Bin window, then close it.
   d. Drag the Recycle Bin to a different corner of the screen, then drag it back to its original location.
   e. Click or tap the Date and Time area to display the calendar and clock, then click or tap it again to close it.

4. **Start an app.**
   a. Open the Start menu, then start the Maps app. (If asked to allow Windows to access your location, do so if you like.)
   b. Click or tap the icons on the left side of the Maps app window and observe the effect of each one.
   c. Close the Maps app.
   d. Reopen the Start menu, then type and click or tap to locate and open the Sticky Notes accessory.
   e. Click or tap the Sticky Notes Close button, clicking or tapping Yes to delete the note.
   f. Open the Weather Windows app.

5. **Work with a window.**
   a. Minimize the Weather window, then use its taskbar button to redisplay the window.
   b. Use the Weather app window's scroll bar or swiping to view the information in the lower part of the window, and then scroll or swipe up to display the top of it. (*Hint*: You need to move the pointer over the Weather app window, or swipe it, in order to display the scroll bar.)
   c. Click or tap the menu expand button, then click Historical Weather.
   d. Read the contents of the window, then click or tap two other menu buttons and read the contents.
   e. Maximize the Weather window, then restore it down.

6. **Manage multiple windows.**
   a. Leaving the Weather app open, go to the Start menu and type to locate the Paint app, open Paint, then restore down the Paint window if necessary.
   b. Click or tap to make the Weather app window the active window.
   c. Click or tap to make the Paint window the active window.
   d. Minimize the Paint window.

Skills Review (continued)

    e. Drag the Weather app window so it's in the middle of the screen.

    f. Redisplay the Paint window.

    g. Drag the Paint window so it automatically fills the right side of the screen.

    h. Click or tap the Weather app window image so it snaps to the left side of the screen.

    i. Close the Weather app window, maximize the Paint window, then restore down the Paint window.

7. Use buttons, menus, and dialog boxes.

FIGURE 1-25

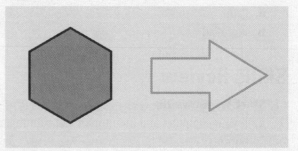

    a. In the Paint window, draw a Dark red Hexagon shape, similar to the one shown in **FIGURE 1-25**.

    b. Use the Fill with color button to fill the hexagon with a brown color.

    c. Draw an Orange right arrow to the right of the hexagon shape, using the figure as a guide.

    d. Use the Fill with color button to fill the orange arrow with a lime color.

    e. Fill the drawing background with Light turquoise color, as shown in the figure.

    f. Use the Select list arrow and menu to select the entire drawing, then use the Rotate command to rotate the drawing 180°.

    g. Open the Print dialog box, print a copy of the picture if you wish, then close the Paint app without saving the drawing.

8. Get help.

    a. Open the Get Started app, then use the menu expand button to display the available help topics.

    b. Use the Menu button to display help for Cortana.

    c. Click or tap a tile representing a Cortana help topic that interests you, read the help text, scrolling or swiping as necessary.

    d. Display the Search and Help topic, then close the Get Started window.

    e. In the search box on the taskbar, type Help Microsoft Account, then click the help Microsoft account result to search the web.

    f. In the Microsoft Edge browser window, select a help topic that interests you, read the information (ignore any commercial offers), then click or tap the Microsoft Edge window's Close button.

9. Exit Windows 10.

    a. Sign out of your account, or shut down your computer using the Shut down command in the Start menu's Power command or the preferred command for your work or school setting.

    b. Turn off your monitor if necessary.

Independent Challenge 1

You work for Chicago Instruments, a manufacturer of brass instruments. The company ships instruments and supplies to music stores and musicians in the United States and Canada. The owner, Emerson, wants to know an easy way for his employees to learn about the new features of Windows 10, and he has asked you to help.

    a. Start your computer if necessary, sign in to Windows 10, then use the search text box to search for **what's new in Windows 10**.

    b. Click or tap the Search the web link in the Best match section at the top of the Help menu, then in the Microsoft Edge browser window, click or tap a search result that interests you.

    c. Open the Getting Started app and review the new features listed there.

    d. Using pencil and paper, or the Notepad accessory if you wish, write a short memo to Emerson summarizing, in your own words, three important new features in Windows 10. If you use Notepad to write the memo, use the Print button to print the document, then use the Exit command on the File tab to close Notepad without saving your changes to the document.

Independent Challenge 1 (continued)

e. Close the browser window, then sign out of your account, or shut down your computer using the preferred command for your work or school setting. Turn off your monitor if necessary.

Independent Challenge 2

You are the new manager of Katharine Anne's Garden Supplies, a business that supplies garden tools to San Diego businesses. Some of their tools are from Europe and show metric sizes. For her American customers, Katharine Anne wants to do a simple calculation and then convert the result to inches.

a. Start your computer and log on to Windows 10 if necessary, then type to locate the Windows app called Calculator, and start it.
b. Click or tap to enter the number 96 on the Calculator.
c. Click or tap the division sign (÷) button.
d. Click or tap the number 4.
e. Click or tap the equals sign button (=), and write down the result shown in the Calculator window. (*Hint*: The result should be 24.)
f. Select the menu expand button in the Calculator window, then under CONVERTER, select Length.
g. Enter 24 centimeters, and observe the equivalent length in inches.
h. Start Notepad, write a short memo about how Calculator can help you convert metric measurements to inches and feet, print the document using the Print command on the File tab, then exit Notepad without saving.
i. Close the Calculator, then sign out of your account, or shut down your computer using the preferred command for your work or school setting. Turn off your monitor if necessary.

Independent Challenge 3

You are the office manager for Erica's Pet Shipping, a service business in Dallas, Texas, that specializes in air shipping of cats and dogs across the United States and Canada. It's important to know the temperature in the destination city, so the animals won't be in danger from extreme temperatures when they are unloaded from the aircraft. Erica has asked you to find a way to easily monitor temperatures in destination cities. You decide to use a Windows app so you can see current temperatures in Celsius on your desktop. (Note: To complete the steps below, your computer must be connected to the Internet.)

a. Start your computer and sign in to Windows 10 if necessary, then on the Start menu, click or tap the Weather tile.
b. Click or tap the Search icon in the location text box, then type **Toronto**.
c. Select Toronto, Ontario, Canada, in the drop-down list to view the weather for Toronto.
d. Search on and select another location that interests you.
e. Close the app.
f. Open Notepad, write Erica a memo outlining how you can use the Windows Weather app to help keep pets safe, print the memo if you wish, close Notepad, then sign out, or shut down your computer.

Independent Challenge 4: Explore

Cortana, the Windows 10 personal digital assistant, can help you with everyday tasks. In this Independent Challenge, you explore one of the ways you can use Cortana.

a. Click or tap the microphone icon, to the right of the search box in the Windows 10 taskbar, to activate Cortana and display its menu. (*Note*: If you have not used Cortana before, you will not see the microphone icon until you answer some preliminary questions and verify your user account; you may also need to first help Cortana to understand your speaking voice.) Cortana displays a pulsating circle, indicating that she is listening for speech, and then shows you a greeting and some general information.

Independent Challenge 4: Explore (continued)

FIGURE 1-26

b. In the list of icons on the left side of the menu, click the menu expand button to show the names of each one, as shown in **FIGURE 1-26**.

c. Click or tap the Reminders button, then click the plus sign at the bottom of the menu. Click or tap Remember to..., then enter information for a to-do item, such as "Walk the dog." Click or tap the time box and use the spin boxes to set the time for one or two minutes from now. Click or tap the check mark, then click Remind to set the reminder. Click or tap the Reminders icon again to see your reminder listed, then click the desktop. When the reminder appears, click Complete.

d. Click or tap the microphone icon again, and when you see the pulsating circle, speak into your computer microphone and tell Cortana to remind you to do something in one minute. Click or tap Remind, then close the Cortana window. When the reminder appears, click or tap Complete.

e. Click or tap the Close button on the Cortana menu, then sign out of your account, or shut down your computer.

Visual Workshop

Using the skills you've learned in this module, open and arrange elements on your screen so it looks similar to **FIGURE 1-27**. Note the position of the Recycle Bin, and the size and location of the Notepad and Weather app windows, as well as the city shown. In Notepad, write a paragraph summarizing how you used pointing, clicking (or tapping), and dragging to make your screen look like the figure. Print your work if you wish, close Notepad and the Weather app without saving changes, then sign out or shut down your computer.

FIGURE 1-27

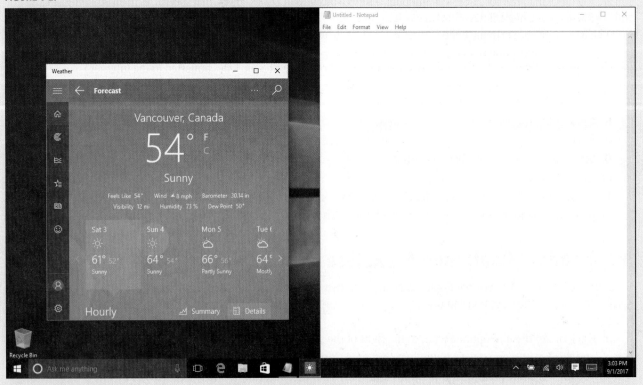

Understanding File Management

CASE Now that you are familiar with the Windows 10 operating system, your new employer has asked you to become familiar with **file management**, or how to create, save, locate and delete the files you create with Windows apps. You begin by reviewing how files are organized on your computer, and then begin working with files you create in the WordPad app. *Note: With the release of Windows 10, Microsoft now provides ongoing updates to Windows instead of releasing new versions periodically. This means that Windows features might change over time, including how they look and how you interact with them. The information provided in this text was accurate at the time this book was published.*

Module Objectives

After completing this module, you will be able to:

- Understand files and folders
- Create and save a file
- Explore the files and folders on your computer
- Change file and folder views

- Open, edit, and save files
- Copy files
- Move and rename files
- Search for files and folders
- Delete and restore files

Files You Will Need

No files needed.

Understand Files and Folders

Learning
Outcomes
• Analyze a file
hierarchy
• Examine files and
folders

As you work with apps, you create and save files, such as letters, drawings, or budgets. When you save files, you usually save them inside folders to help keep them organized. The files and folders on your computer are organized in a **file hierarchy**, a system that arranges files and folders in different levels, like the branches of a tree. **FIGURE 2-1** shows a sample file hierarchy. **CASE** ▶ *You decide to use folders and files to organize the information on your computer.*

DETAILS

Use the following guidelines as you organize files using your computer's file hierarchy:

- **Use folders and subfolders to organize files**

  As you work with your computer, you can add folders to your hierarchy and name them to help you organize your work. As you've learned, folders are storage areas in which you can group related files. You should give folders unique names that help you easily identify them. You can also create **subfolders**, which are folders that are inside other folders. Windows 10 comes with several existing folders, such as Documents, Music, Pictures, and Videos, that you can use as a starting point.

QUICK TIP

When you open File Explorer, you see a list of recently opened files and frequently used folders in the Quick Access area that helps you go directly to files and locations.

- **View and manage files in File Explorer**

  You can view and manage your computer contents using a built-in program called **File Explorer**, shown in **FIGURE 2-2**. A File Explorer window is divided into **panes**, or sections. The **Navigation pane** on the left side of the window shows the folder structure on your computer. When you click a folder in the Navigation pane, you see its contents in the **File list** on the right side of the window. To open File Explorer from the desktop, click the File Explorer button ▣ on the taskbar. To open it from the Start menu, click the File Explorer shortcut.

QUICK TIP

The name "File Explorer" only appears in the title bar when you first open it. As you navigate, you'll see the current folder name instead.

- **Understand file addresses**

  A window also contains an **Address bar**, an area just below the Ribbon that shows the address, or location, of the files that appear in the File list. An **address** is a sequence of folder names, separated by the ▶ symbol, which describes a file's location in the file hierarchy. An address shows the folder with the highest hierarchy level on the left and steps through each hierarchy level toward the right; this is sometimes called a **path**. For example, the Documents folder might contain subfolders named Work and Personal. If you clicked the Personal folder in the File list, the Address bar would show Documents ▶ Personal. Each location between the ▶ symbols represents a level in the file hierarchy. If you see a file path written out, you'll most likely see it with backslashes. For example, in **FIGURE 2-1**, if you wanted to write the path to the Brochure file, you would write "Documents\Reason2Go\Marketing\Brochure.xlsx. File addresses might look complicated if they may have many levels, but they are helpful because they always describe the exact location of a file or folder in a file hierarchy.

QUICK TIP

Remember that in the Address bar and Navigation pane you single-click a folder or subfolder to show its contents, but in the File list you double-click it.

- **Navigate up and down using the Address bar and File list**

  You can use the Address bar and the File list to move up or down in the hierarchy one or more levels at a time. To **navigate up** in your computer's hierarchy, you can click a folder or subfolder name to the left of the current folder name in the Address bar. For example, in **FIGURE 2-2**, you can move up in the hierarchy three levels by clicking once on This PC in the Address bar. Then the File list would show the subfolders and files inside the This PC folder. To **navigate down** in the hierarchy, double-click a subfolder in the File list. The path in the Address bar then shows the path to that subfolder.

- **Navigate up and down using the Navigation pane**

  You can also use the Navigation pane to navigate among folders. Move the mouse pointer over the Navigation pane, then click the small arrows to the left of a folder name to show ▶ or hide ▼ the folder's contents under the folder name. Subfolders appear indented under the folders that contain them, showing that they are inside that folder.

Understanding File Management

FIGURE 2-1: Sample folder and file hierarchy

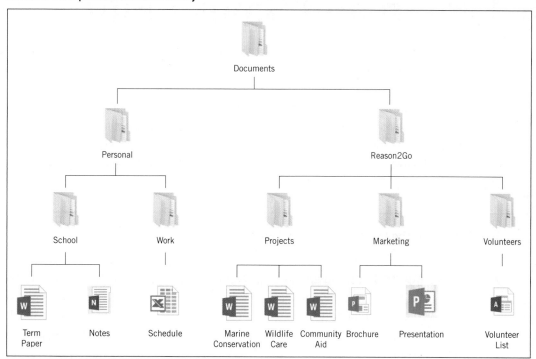

FIGURE 2-2: File Explorer window

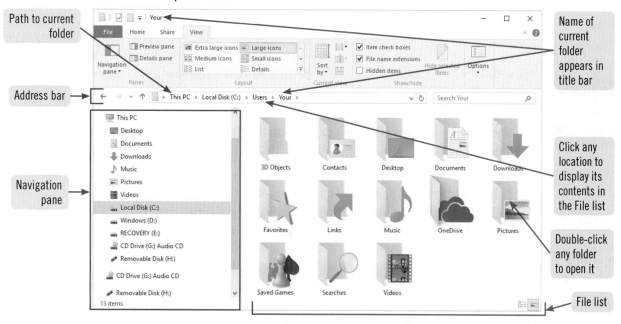

Plan your file organization

As you manage your files, you should plan how you want to organize them. First, identify the types of files you work with, such as images, music, and documents. Think about the content, such as personal, business, clients, or projects. Then think of a folder organization that will help you find them later. For example, you can use subfolders in the Pictures folder to separate family photos from business photos or to group them by location or by month. In the Documents folder, you might group personal files in one subfolder and business files in another subfolder. Then create additional subfolders to further separate sets of files. You can always move files among folders and rename folders. You should periodically reevaluate your folder structure to make sure it continues to meet your needs.

Create and Save a File

Learning
Outcomes
• Start WordPad
• Create a file
• Save a file

After you start a program and create a new file, the file exists only in your computer's **random access memory (RAM)**, a temporary storage location. RAM contains information only when your computer is on. When you turn off your computer, it automatically clears the contents of RAM. So you need to save a new file onto a storage device that permanently stores the file so you can open, change, and use it later. One important storage device is your computer's hard drive built into your computer. You might want to store your files online in an online storage location like Microsoft OneDrive. Or you might use a **USB flash drive**, a small, portable storage device that you plug into a USB port on your computer. **CASE** *You create a document, then save it.*

STEPS

1. **Click or tap the Start button, then type** word

   Available apps with "word" in their names are listed. See **FIGURE 2-3**.

2. **Click the** WordPad Desktop app listing, **then maximize the WordPad window if necessary**

   Near the top of the WordPad window you see the Ribbon containing buttons, similar to those you used in Paint in Module 1. The Home tab appears in front. A new, blank document appears in the document window. The blinking insertion point shows you where the next character you type will appear.

3. **Type** Company Overview, **then press** [Enter] **twice, type** Conservation, **press** [Enter], **type** Community Work, **press** [Enter], **type** Research, **press** [Enter] **twice, then type your name**

   See **FIGURE 2-4**.

4. **Click the** File tab, **then click** Save

   The first time you save a file using the Save button, the Save As dialog box opens. You use this dialog box to name the file and choose a storage location for it. The Save As dialog box has many of the same elements as a File Explorer window, including an Address bar, a Navigation pane, and a File list. Below the Address bar, the **toolbar** contains buttons you can click to perform actions. In the Address bar, you can see the Documents folder, which is the **default**, or automatically selected, storage location. But you can easily change it.

5. **If you are saving to a USB flash drive, plug the drive into a USB port on your computer, if necessary**

6. **In the Navigation pane scroll bar, click the** down scroll arrow ☑ **as needed to see This PC and any storage devices listed under it**

   Under This PC, you see the storage locations available on your computer, such as Local Disk (C:) (your hard drive) and Removable Disk (H:) (your USB drive name and letter might differ). Above This PC, you might see your OneDrive listed. These storage locations are like folders in that you can open them and store files in them.

7. **Click the name of your USB flash drive, or the folder where you store your Data Files**

   The files and folders in the location you chose, if any, appear in the File list. The Address bar shows the location where the file will be saved, which is now Removable Disk (H:) or the name of the location you clicked. You need to give your document a meaningful name so you can find it later.

8. **Click in the** File name text box **to select the default name** Document.rtf, **type** Company Overview, **compare your screen to** FIGURE 2-5, **then click** Save

   The document is saved as a file on your USB flash drive. The filename Company Overview.rtf appears in the title bar. The ".rtf" at the end of the filename is the file extension that Windows added automatically. A **file extension** is a three- or four-letter sequence, preceded by a period, which identifies a file to your computer, in this case **Rich Text Format**. The WordPad program creates files in RTF format.

9. **Click the** Close button ☒ **on the WordPad window**

   The WordPad program closes. Your Company Overview document is now saved in the location you specified.

Understanding File Management

FIGURE 2-3: Results at top of Start menu

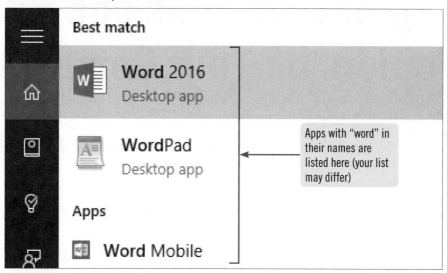

Apps with "word" in their names are listed here (your list may differ)

FIGURE 2-4: WordPad document

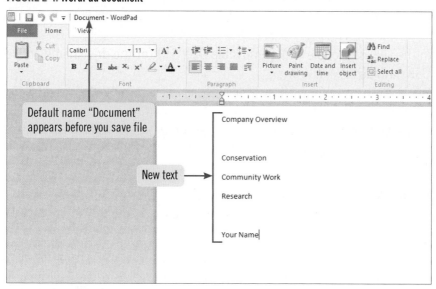

Default name "Document" appears before you save file

New text

FIGURE 2-5: Save As dialog box

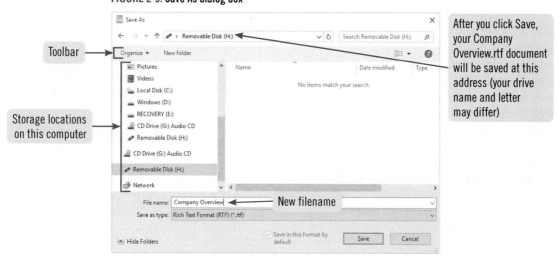

Toolbar

Storage locations on this computer

After you click Save, your Company Overview.rtf document will be saved at this address (your drive name and letter may differ)

New filename

Understanding File Management

Explore the Files and Folders on Your Computer

In a File Explorer window, you can navigate through your computer contents using the File list, the Address bar, and the Navigation pane. Examining your computer and its existing folder and file structure helps you decide where to save files as you work with Windows 10 apps.   **CASE** ▶ *In preparation for organizing documents at your new job, you look at the files and folders on your computer.*

STEPS

1. **At the Windows desktop, click the File Explorer button 📁 on the taskbar, then in the File Explorer Navigation pane, click This PC**

TROUBLE

If you don't see the colored bars, click the View tab, click Tiles in the Layout group.

2. **If you do not see a band of buttons near the top of the window, double-click the View tab**

   The band containing buttons is called the **Ribbon**. Your computer's storage devices appear in a window, as shown in **FIGURE 2-6**. These include hard drives; devices with removable storage, such as CD and DVD drives or USB flash drives; portable devices such as smartphones or tablets; and any network storage locations. Colored bars shows you how much space has been taken up on your drives. You decide to move down a level in your computer's hierarchy and see what is on your USB flash drive.

3. **In the File list, double-click Removable Disk (H:) (or the drive name and letter for your USB flash drive)**

   You see the contents of your USB flash drive, including the Company Overview.rtf file you saved in the last lesson. You decide to navigate one level up in the file hierarchy.

TROUBLE

If you do not have a USB flash drive, click the Documents folder instead.

4. **In the Address bar, click This PC, or if This PC does not appear, click the far-left address bar arrow ▶ in the Address bar, then click This PC**

   You return to the This PC window showing your storage locations.

5. **In the File list, double-click Local Disk (C:)**

   The contents of your hard drive appear in the File list.

6. **In the File list, double-click the Users folder**

   The Users folder contains a subfolder for each user account on this computer. You might see a folder with your user account name on it. Each user's folder contains that person's documents. User folder names are the names that were used to log in when your computer was set up. When a user logs in, the computer allows that user access to the folder with the same user name. If you are using a computer with more than one user, you might not have permission to view other users' folders. There is also a Public folder that any user can open.

7. **Double-click the folder with your user name on it**

   Depending on how your computer is set up, this folder might be labeled with your name; however, if you are using a computer in a lab or a public location, your folder might be called Student or Computer User or something similar. You see a list of folders, such as Documents, Music, and OneDrive. See **FIGURE 2-7**.

QUICK TIP

In the Address bar, you can click ▶ to the right of a folder name to see a list of its subfolders; if the folder is open, its name appears in bold in the list.

8. **Double-click Documents in the File list**

   In the Address bar, the path to the Documents folder is This PC ▶ Local Disk (C:) ▶ Users ▶ *Your User Name* ▶ Documents.

9. **In the Navigation pane, click This PC**

   You once again see your computer's storage locations. You can also move up one level at a time in your file hierarchy by clicking the Up arrow ⬆ on the toolbar, or by pressing [Backspace] on your keyboard. See **TABLE 2-1** for a summary of techniques for navigating through your computer's file hierarchy.

FIGURE 2-6: File Explorer window showing storage locations

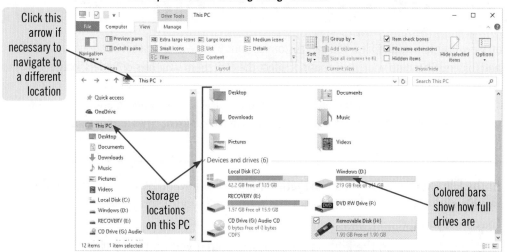

Click this arrow if necessary to navigate to a different location

Storage locations on this PC

Colored bars show how full drives are

FIGURE 2-7: Your user name folder

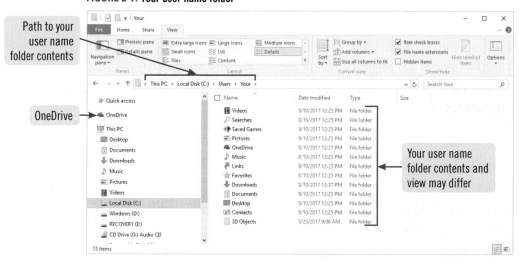

Path to your user name folder contents

OneDrive

Your user name folder contents and view may differ

TABLE 2-1: Navigating your computer's file hierarchy

to do this	Navigation pane	Address bar	File list	keyboard
Move up in hierarchy	Click a drive or folder name	Click an item to the left of [>] or Click the **Up to** button [↑]		Press **[Backspace]**
Move down in hierarchy	Click a drive or folder name that is indented from the left	Click an item to the right of [>]	Double-click a folder	Press [↑] or [↓] to select a folder, then press **[Enter]** to open the selected folder
Return to previously viewed location		Click the **Back to** button [←] or **Forward** button [→]		

Using and disabling Quick Access view

When you first open File Explorer, you see a list of frequently-used folders and recently used files, called Quick access view. Quick Access view can save you time by giving you one-click access to files and folders you use a lot. If you want File Explorer to open instead to This PC, you can disable Quick Access View. To do this, open a File Explorer window, click the View tab, click the Options button on the right side of the Ribbon, then click Change folder and search options. On the General tab of the Folder Options dialog box, click the Open File Explorer to list arrow, click This PC, then click OK.

Change File and Folder Views

Learning Outcomes
- View files as large icons
- Sort files
- Preview files

As you view your folders and files, you can customize your **view**, which is a set of appearance choices for files and folders. Changing your view does not affect the content of your files or folders, only the way they appear. You can choose from eight different **layouts** to display your folders and files as different sized icons, or as a list. You can change the order in which the folders and files appear, and you can also show a preview of a file in the window. **CASE** > *You experiment with different views of your folders and files.*

STEPS

QUICK TIP
To expand your view of a location in the Navigation pane, click the Expand button ⟩ next to that location.

1. **In the File Explorer window's Navigation pane, click Local Disk (C:); in the File list double-click Users, then double-click the folder with your user name**
   You opened your user name folder, which is inside the Users folder.

2. **Click the View tab on the Ribbon if necessary, then if you don't see eight icons in the Layout list, click the More button ▼ in the Layout group**
   The list of available layouts appears, as shown in **FIGURE 2-8**.

3. **Click Extra large icons in the Layout list**
   In this view, the folder items appear as very large icons in the File list. This layout is especially helpful for image files, because you can see what the pictures are without opening each one.

QUICK TIP
You can scroll up and down in the Layout group to see views that are not currently visible.

4. **On the View tab, in the Layout list, point to the other layouts while watching the appearance of the File list, then click Details**
   In Details view, shown in **FIGURE 2-9**, you can see each item's name, the date it was modified, and its file type. It shows the size of any files in the current folder, but it does not show sizes for folders.

5. **Click the Sort by button in the Current view group**
   The Sort by menu lets you **sort**, or reorder, your files and folders according to several criteria.

6. **Click Descending if it is not already selected with a check mark**
   Now the folders are sorted in reverse alphabetical order.

QUICK TIP
Clicking Quick Access in the Navigation pane displays folders you use frequently; to add a folder or location to Quick Access, display it in the File list, then drag it to the Quick Access list.

7. **Click Removable Disk (H:) (or the location where you store your Data Files) in the Navigation pane, then click Company Overview.rtf in the File list**

8. **Click the Preview pane button in the Panes group on the View tab if necessary**
   A preview of the selected Company Overview.rtf file you created earlier appears in the Preview pane on the right side of the screen. The WordPad file is not open, but you can still see the file's contents. See **FIGURE 2-10**.

9. **Click the Preview pane button again to close the pane, then click the window's Close button ✕**

Using the Windows Action Center

The Windows Action Center lets you quickly view system notifications and selected computer settings. To open the Action Center, click the Notifications button on the right side of the taskbar. The Action Center pane opens on the right side of the screen. Any new notifications appear in the upper part of the pane, including messages about apps, Windows tips, and any reminders you may have set. In the lower part of the pane, you see Quick Action buttons, shown in **FIGURE 2-11**, for some commonly-used Windows settings. For example, click Note to open the OneNote app; click the Brightness button repeatedly to cycle though four brightness settings; click the Airplane mode button to place your computer in airplane mode,

which turns off your computer's wireless transmission; click Quiet hours to silence your computer's notification sounds. Clicking the All settings button opens the Settings windows, where you can access all Windows settings categories. Note that the buttons available will vary depending on your hardware and software configuration.

FIGURE 2-11: Quick Action buttons

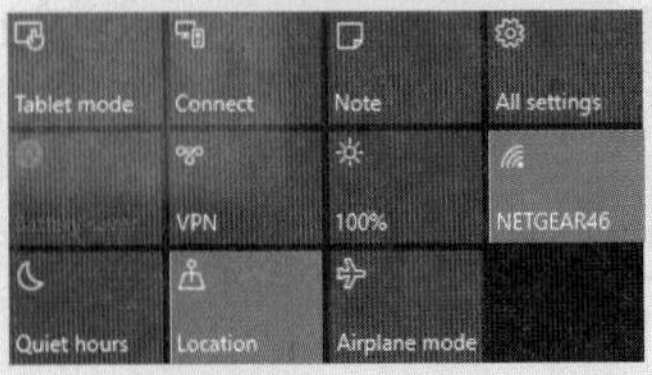

FIGURE 2-8: Layout options for viewing folders and files

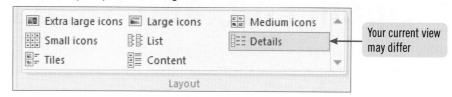

FIGURE 2-9: Your user name folder contents in Details view

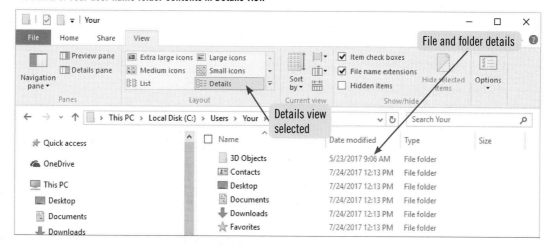

FIGURE 2-10: Preview of selected Company Overview.rtf file

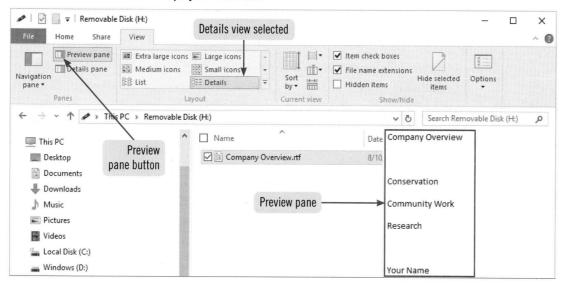

Customizing Details view

When you use File Explorer to view your computer contents in Details view, you see a list of the files and folders in that location. At the top of the list you see each item's Name, Size, Type, and Date Modified. If the list of file and folder details doesn't show what you need, you can customize it. To change a column's location, drag a column heading to move it quickly to a new position. To change the order of, or **sort**, your files and folders, click any column header to sort the list by that detail; click it a second time column header to sort the list by that detail; click it a second time to reverse the order. To show only a selected group of, or **filter**, files, click the ![icon] icon to the right of the Name, Size, Type, or Date Modified, column headers, and select the check boxes for the type of items you want to include. To change the kind of details you see, right-click or tap-hold a column heading in Details view, then click or tap the detail you want to show or hide. To see more details or to change the list order, right-click or tap-hold a column title, then click or tap More.

Understanding File Management

Windows 10

Open, Edit, and Save Files

Learning
Outcomes
• Open a file
• Edit a file
• Save a file

Once you have created a file and saved it with a name to a storage location, you can easily open it and **edit** (make changes to) it. For example, you might want to add or delete text or add a picture. Then you save the file again so the file contains your latest changes. Usually you save a file with the same filename and in the same location as the original, which replaces the existing file with the most up-to-date version. To save a file you have changed, you use the Save command. **CASE** ▶ *You need to complete the company overview list, so you need to open the new Company Overview file you created earlier.*

STEPS

QUICK TIP

When you double-click a file in a File Explorer window, the program currently associated with that file type opens the file; to change the program, right-click a file, click Open with, click Choose another app, click the program name, select the Always use this app to open [file type] files check box, then click OK.

1. **Click the** Start button, **begin typing** wordpad, **then click the** WordPad program **if it is not selected or, if it is, simply press [Enter]**
   The WordPad program opens on the desktop.

2. **Click the** File tab, **then click** Open
   The Open dialog box opens. It contains a Navigation pane and a File list like the Save As dialog box and the File Explorer window.

3. **Scroll down in the Navigation pane if necessary until you see This PC and the list of computer locations, then click** Removable Disk (H:) **(or the location where you store your Data Files)**
   The contents of your USB flash drive (or the file storage location you chose) appear in the File list, as shown in **FIGURE 2-12**.

QUICK TIP

You can also double-click a file in the File list to open it.

4. **Click** Company Overview.rtf **in the File list, then click** Open
   The document you created earlier opens.

5. **Click to the right of the "h" in Research, press [Enter], then type** Outreach
   The edited document includes the text you just typed. See **FIGURE 2-13**.

QUICK TIP

To save changes to a file, you can also click the Save button 💾 on the Quick Access toolbar (on the left side of the title bar).

6. **Click the** File tab, **then click** Save, **as shown in** FIGURE 2-14
   WordPad saves the document with your most recent changes, using the filename and location you specified when you previously saved it. When you save changes to an existing file, the Save As dialog box does not open.

7. **Click the** File tab, **then click** Exit
   The Company Overview document and the WordPad program close.

Comparing Save and Save As

Many apps, including Wordpad, include two save command options—Save and Save As. The first time you save a file, the Save As dialog box opens (whether you choose Save or Save As). Here you can select the drive and folder where you want to save the file and enter its filename. If you edit a previously saved file, you can save the file to the same location with the same file-name using the Save command. The Save command updates the stored file using the same location and filename without opening the Save As dialog box. In some situations, you might want to save a copy of the existing document using a different filename or in a different storage location. To do this, open the document, click the Save As command on the File tab, navigate to the location where you want to save the copy if necessary, and/or edit the name of the file.

FIGURE 2-12: Navigating in the Open dialog box

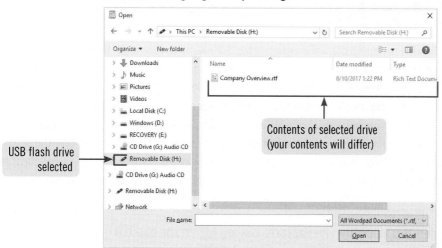

USB flash drive selected

Contents of selected drive (your contents will differ)

FIGURE 2-13: Edited document

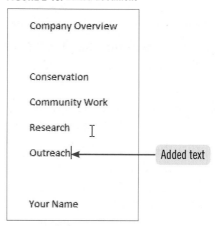

Added text

FIGURE 2-14: Saving the updated document

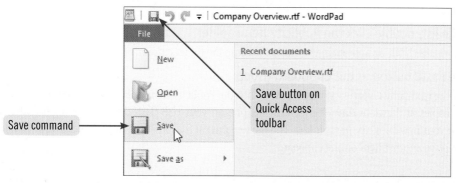

Save command

Save button on Quick Access toolbar

Using Microsoft OneDrive

Microsoft OneDrive is a location on the World Wide Web where you can store your files. Because OneDrive is an online location instead of a disk or USB device, it's often called a **cloud storage location**. When you store your files on OneDrive, you can access them from different devices, including laptops, tablets, and smartphones. Any changes you make to a file stored "in the cloud" are automatically made on OneDrive; this is known as **file syncing**. For example, if you make changes to a file from your laptop, and then open it on your tablet, you will see the changes. You can share OneDrive folders with others so they can view or edit files using a web browser such as Microsoft Edge or Internet Explorer. You can even have multiple users edit a document simultaneously. In Windows 10, OneDrive appears as a storage location in the navigation bar in File Explorer, and in the Open and Save As dialog boxes in Windows apps, so you can easily open, modify, and save files stored there. You can also download the free OneDrive Windows app from the Windows Store to help manage your OneDrive files from all your devices.

Copy Files

Learning
Outcomes
• Create a new
  folder
• Copy and paste
  a file

Sometimes you need to make a copy of an existing file. For example, you might want to put a copy on a USB flash drive so you can open the file on another machine or share it with a friend or colleague. Or you might want to create a copy as a **backup**, or replacement, in case something happens to your original file. You can copy files and folders using the Copy command and then place the copy in another location using the Paste command. You cannot have two copies of a file with the same name in the same folder. If you try to do this, Windows asks you if you want to replace the first one, and then gives you a chance to give the second copy a different name. **CASE** *You want to create a backup copy of the Company Overview document that you can store in a folder for company publicity items. First you need to create the folder, then you can copy the file.*

STEPS

1. **On the desktop, click the File Explorer button** 🗖 **on the taskbar**

2. **In the Navigation pane, click Removable Disk (H:) (or the location where you store your Data Files)**
   First you create the new folder you plan to use for storing publicity-related files.

3. **In the New group on the Home tab, click the New folder button**
   A new folder appears in the File list, with its default name, New folder, selected.

4. **Type Publicity Items, then press [Enter]**
   Because the folder name was selected, the text you typed, Publicity Items, replaced it. Pressing [Enter] confirmed your entry, and the folder is now named Publicity Items.

5. **In the File list, click the Company Overview.rtf document you saved earlier, then click the Copy button in the Clipboard group, as shown in FIGURE 2-15**
   After you select the file, its check box becomes selected (the check box appears only if the Item check boxes option in the Show/Hide group on the View tab is selected). When you use the Copy command, Windows places a duplicate copy of the file in an area of your computer's random access memory called the **clipboard**, ready to paste, or place, in a new location. Copying and pasting a file leaves the file in its original location.

6. **In the File list, double-click the Publicity Items folder**
   The folder opens. Nothing appears in the File list because the folder currently is empty.

7. **Click the Paste button in the Clipboard group**
   A copy of the Company Overview.rtf file is pasted into the Publicity Items folder. See **FIGURE 2-16**. You now have two copies of the Company Overview.rtf file: one on your USB flash drive in the main folder, and another in your new Publicity Items folder. The file remains on the clipboard until you end your Windows session or place another item on the clipboard.

Copying files using Send to

You can also copy and paste a file using the Send to command. In File Explorer, right-click the file you want to copy, point to Send to, then in the shortcut menu, click the name of the device you want to send a copy of the file to. This leaves the original file on your hard drive and creates a copy in that location. You can send a file to a compressed file, the desktop, your Documents folder, a mail recipient, or a drive on your computer. See **TABLE 2-2**.

FIGURE 2-15: Copying a file

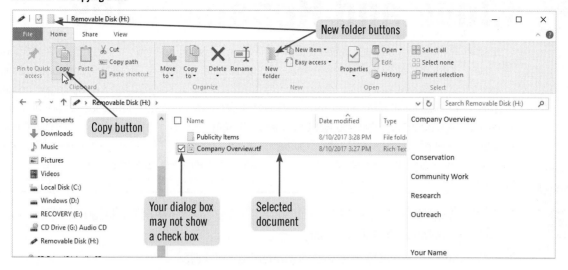

FIGURE 2-16: Duplicate file pasted into Publicity items folder

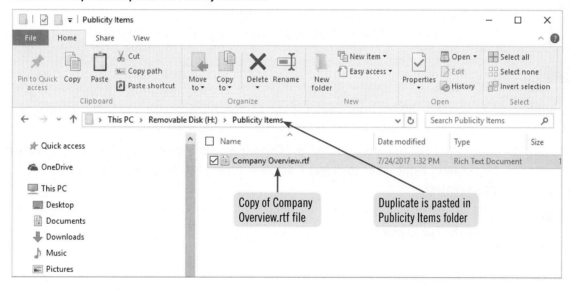

TABLE 2-2: Selected Send to menu commands

menu option	use to
Compressed (zipped) folder	Create a new, compressed (smaller) file with a .zip file extension
Desktop (create shortcut)	Create a shortcut (link) for the file on the desktop
Documents	Copy the file to the Documents library
Fax recipient	Send a file to a fax recipient
Mail recipient	Create an e-mail with the file attached to it (only if you have an e-mail program on your computer)
DVD RW Drive (D:)	Copy the file to your computer's DVD drive (your drive letter may differ)
CD Drive (G:) audio CD	Copy the file to your computer's CD drive (your drive letter may differ)
Removable Disk (H:)	Copy the file to a removable disk drive (your drive letter may differ)

Move and Rename Files

Learning Outcomes
• Cut and paste a file
• Rename a file

As you work with files, you might need to move files or folders to another location. You can move one or more files or folders at a time, and you can move them to a different folder on the same drive or to a different drive. When you **move** a file, the file is transferred to the new location, and unlike copying, it no longer exists in its original location. You can move a file using the Cut and Paste commands. Before or after you move a file, you might find that you want to change its name. You can easily rename it to make the name more descriptive or accurate. **CASE ▶** *You decide to move your original Company Overview.rtf document to your Documents folder. After you move it, you edit the filename so it better describes the file contents.*

STEPS

1. **In the Address bar, click Removable Disk (H:) (or the name of the location where you store your Data Files) if necessary**

2. **Click the Company Overview.rtf document to select it**

3. **Click the Cut button in the Clipboard group on the Ribbon, as shown in FIGURE 2-17**

4. **In the Navigation Pane, under This PC, click Documents**
   You navigated to your Documents folder.

5. **Click the Paste button in the Clipboard group**
   The Company Overview.rtf document appears in your Documents folder and remains selected. See **FIGURE 2-18**. The filename could be clearer, to help you remember that it contains a list of company goals.

6. **With the Company Overview.rtf file selected, click the Rename button in the Organize group**
   The filename is highlighted. The file extension isn't highlighted because that part of the filename identifies the file to WordPad and should not be changed. If you deleted or changed the file extension, WordPad would be unable to open the file. You decide to change the word "Overview" to "Goals."

7. **Move the I pointer after the "w" in "Overview", click to place the insertion point, press [Backspace] eight times to delete Overview, type Goals as shown in FIGURE 2-19, then press [Enter]**
   You changed the name of the pasted file in the Documents folder. The filename now reads Company Goals.rtf.

8. **Close the File Explorer window**

Using Task View to create multiple desktops

As you have learned in Module 1, you can have multiple app windows open on your desktop, such as WordPad, Paint, and OneNote. But you might need to have a different set of apps available for a different project. Instead of closing all the apps and opening different ones, you can use Task View to work with multiple desktops, each containing its own set of apps. Then, when you need to work on another project, you can switch to another desktop to quickly access those apps. To open Task View, click the **Task View** button 🔲 on the taskbar. The current desktop becomes smaller and a New desktop button appears in the lower-right corner of the screen. Click the New desktop button. A new desktop appears in a bar at the bottom of the screen, which you can click to activate and work with its

apps. See **FIGURE 2-20**. To switch to another desktop, click the Task View button and click its icon.

FIGURE 2-20: Working with multiple desktops in Task view

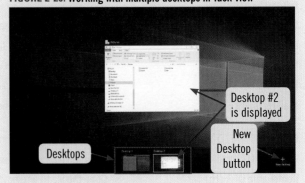

Desktop #2 is displayed

New Desktop button

Desktops

FIGURE 2-17: Cutting a file

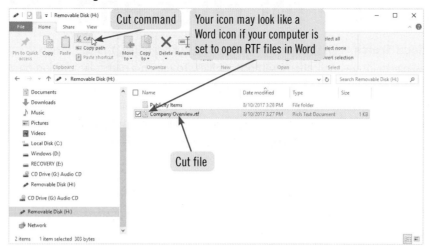

FIGURE 2-18: Pasted file in Documents folder

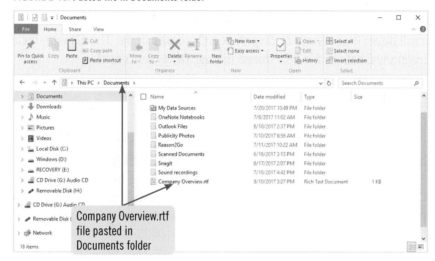

FIGURE 2-19: Renaming a file

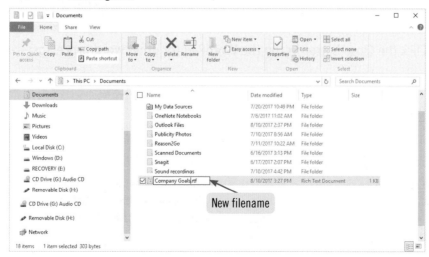

Search for Files and Folders

Learning
Outcomes
• Search for a file
• Open a found file

Windows Search helps you quickly find any app, folder, or file. You can search from the Search box on the taskbar to locate applications, settings, or files. To search a particular location on your computer, you can use the Search box in File Explorer. You enter search text by typing one or more letter sequences or words that help Windows identify the item you want. The search text you type is called your **search criteria.** Your search criteria can be a folder name, a filename, or part of a filename. **CASE** *You want to locate the Company Overview.rtf document so you can print it for a colleague.*

STEPS

1. **Click in the search box on the taskbar**
   The Cortana menu opens.

2. **Type company**
   The Search menu opens with a possible match for your search at the top, and some other possible matches below it. You may see results from The Windows Store, the Internet, or your computer settings.

3. **Click My stuff, near the bottom of the menu**
   This limits your search to the files and folders in your storage locations on this device. It includes documents with the text "company" in the title or in the document text.

QUICK TIP
If you navigate to a specific folder in your file hierarchy, Windows searches that folder and any subfolders below it.

4. **Scroll down if necessary to display search results under This Device, including the Company Goals.rtf file you stored in your Documents folder**
   See FIGURE 2-21. It does not find the Company Overview.rtf file stored on your Flash drive because it's searching only the items on this device. To open the found file, you could click its listing. You can also search using File Explorer.

5. **Click the File Explorer button ▣ on the taskbar, then click This PC in the Navigation pane**

QUICK TIP
Windows search is not case-sensitive, so you can type upper- or lowercase letters, and obtain the same results.

6. **Click in the Search This PC box to the right of the Address bar, type company, then press [Enter]**
   Windows searches your computer for files that contain the word "company" in their title. A green bar in the Address bar indicates the progress of your search. After a few moments, the search results, shown in FIGURE 2-22, appear. Windows found the renamed file, Company Goals.rtf, in your Documents folder, and the original Company Overview.rtf document on your removable drive, in the Publicity Items folder. It may also locate shortcuts to the file in your Recent folder. It's good to verify the location of the found files, so you can select the right one.

7. **Click the View tab, click Details in the Layout group then look in the Folder column to view the path to each file, dragging the edge of the Folder column header with the ↔ pointer to widen it if necessary**

TROUBLE
If you see a message asking how you want to open the file, click WordPad.

8. **Double-click the Company Overview.rtf document in your file storage location**
   The file opens in WordPad or in another word-processing program on your computer that reads RTF files.

9. **Click the Close button ☒ on the WordPad (or other word-processor) window**

Using the Search Tools tab in File Explorer

The **Search Tools tab** appears in the Ribbon as soon as you click the Search text box, and it lets you narrow your search criteria. Use the commands in the Location group to specify a particular search location. The Refine group lets you limit the search to files modified after a certain date, or to files of a particular kind, size, type, or other property. The Options group lets you repeat previous searches, save searches, and open the folder containing a found file.

FIGURE 2-21: Found file

Found documents show path and some text

Your search results will differ

FIGURE 2-22: Apps screen and Search pane

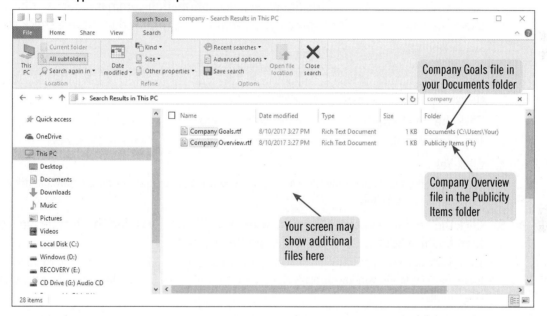

Company Goals file in your Documents folder

Company Overview file in the Publicity Items folder

Your screen may show additional files here

Using Microsoft Edge

When you search for files using the search box on the Windows taskbar and click Web, the new web browser called **Microsoft Edge** opens. You can also open Edge by clicking its icon 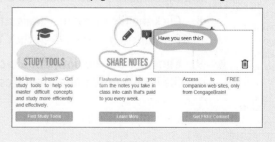 on the taskbar. Created to replace the older Internet Explorer browser, Edge is a Windows app that runs on personal computers, tablets, and smartphones. Edge features a reading mode that lets you read a webpage without ads. It also lets you annotate pages with markup tools such as a pen or highlighter, and add typed notes, as shown in **FIGURE 2-23**. You can also add pages to a Reading list or share them with OneNote or a social networking site.

FIGURE 2-23: Web page annotated in Microsoft Edge

Delete and Restore Files

Learning Outcomes
- Delete a file
- Restore a file
- Empty the Recycle Bin

If you no longer need a folder or file, you can delete (or remove) it from the storage device. By regularly deleting files and folders you no longer need and emptying the Recycle Bin, you free up valuable storage space on your computer. Windows places folders and files you delete from your hard drive in the Recycle Bin. If you delete a folder, Windows removes the folder as well as all files and subfolders stored in it. If you later discover that you need a deleted file or folder, you can restore it to its original location, as long as you have not yet emptied the Recycle Bin. Emptying the Recycle Bin permanently removes deleted folders and files from your computer. However, files and folders you delete from a removable drive, such as a USB flash drive, do not go to the Recycle Bin. They are immediately and permanently deleted and cannot be restored. **CASE** ▸ *You decide to delete the Company Goals document that you stored in your Documents folder.*

STEPS

1. **Click the Documents folder in the File Explorer Navigation pane**
   Your Documents folder opens.

2. **Click Company Goals.rtf to select it, click the Home tab, then click the Delete list arrow ⊠ in the Organize group; if the Show recycle confirmation command does not have a check mark next to it, click Show recycle confirmation (or if it does have a check mark, click ⊠ again to close the menu)**
   Selecting the Show recycle confirmation command tells Windows that whenever you click the Delete button, you want to see a confirmation dialog box before Windows deletes the file. That way you can change your mind if you want, before deleting the file.

3. **Click the Delete button ⊠ in the Organize group**
   The Delete File dialog box opens so you can confirm the deletion, as shown in **FIGURE 2-24**.

4. **Click Yes**
   You deleted the file. Because the file was stored on your computer and not on a removable drive, it was moved to the Recycle Bin.

5. **Click the Minimize button ▭ on the window's title bar, examine the Recycle Bin icon, then double-click the Recycle Bin icon on the desktop**
   The Recycle Bin icon appears to contain crumpled paper, indicating that it contains deleted folders and/or files. The Recycle Bin window displays any previously deleted folders and files, including the Company Goals.rtf file.

6. **Click the Company Goals.rtf file to select it, then click the Restore the selected items button in the Restore group on the Recycle Bin Tools Manage tab, as shown in** FIGURE 2-25
   The file returns to its original location and no longer appears in the Recycle Bin window.

7. **In the Navigation pane, click the Documents folder**
   The Documents folder window contains the restored file. You decide to permanently delete this file after all.

8. **Click the file Company Goals.rtf, click ⊠ in the Organize group on the Home tab, click Permanently delete, then click Yes in the Delete File dialog box**

9. **Minimize the window, double-click the Recycle Bin, notice that the Company Goals.rtf file is no longer there, then close all open windows**

FIGURE 2-24: Delete File dialog box

FIGURE 2-25: Restoring a file from the Recycle Bin

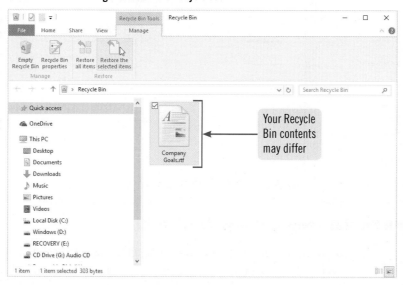

Your Recycle Bin contents may differ

More techniques for selecting and moving files

To select a group of items that are next to each other in a window, click the first item in the group, press and hold [Shift], then click the last item in the group. Both items you click and all the items between them become selected. To select files that are not next to each other, click the first file, press and hold [Ctrl], then click the other items you want to select as a group. Then you can copy, cut, or delete the group of files or folders you selected. **Drag and drop** is a technique in which you use your pointing device to drag a file or folder into a different folder and then drop it, or let go of the mouse button, to place it in that folder. Using drag and drop does not copy your file to the clipboard. If you drag and drop a file to a folder on a different drive, Windows *copies* the file. However, if you drag and drop a file to a folder on the same drive, Windows *moves* the file into that folder

instead. See **FIGURE 2-26**. If you want to move a file to another drive, hold down [Shift] while you drag and drop. If you want to copy a file to another folder on the same drive, hold down [Ctrl] while you drag and drop.

FIGURE 2-26: Moving a file using drag and drop

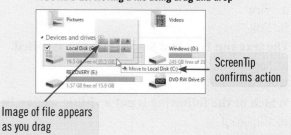

ScreenTip confirms action

Image of file appears as you drag

Windows 10

Practice

Concepts Review

Label the elements of the Windows 10 window shown in FIGURE 2-27.

FIGURE 2-27

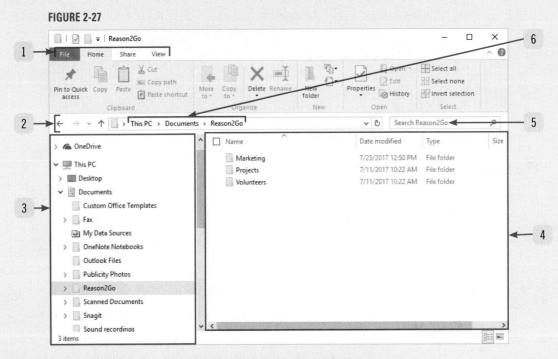

Match each term with the statement that best describes it.

7. **View**
8. **File extension**
9. **Address bar**
10. **Path**
11. **Clipboard**
12. **Snap Assist**

a. A series of locations separated by small triangles or backslashes that describes a file's location in the file hierarchy

b. A feature that helps you arrange windows on the screen

c. An area above the Files list that contains a path

d. A three- or four-letter sequence, preceded by a period, that identifies the type of file

e. A set of appearance choices for files and folders

f. An area of a computer's RAM used for temporary storage

Select the best answer from the list of choices.

13. **Which part of a window lets you see a file's contents without opening the file?**
   a. File list
   b. Address bar
   c. Navigation pane
   d. Preview pane

14. **The new Microsoft web browser is called Microsoft _____.**
   a. View
   b. Task
   c. Edge
   d. Desktop

15. **The text you type in a Search text box is called:**
   a. Sorting.
   b. RAM.
   c. Search criteria.
   d. Clipboard.

16. **Which of the following is not a visible section in a File Explorer window?**
   a. Clipboard
   b. Navigation pane
   c. File list
   d. Address bar

Skills Review

1. **Understand files and folders.**
   a. Create a file hierarchy for an ice cream manufacturing business, using a name that you create. The business has departments for Product Development, Manufacturing, and Personnel. Product development activities include research and testing; manufacturing has facilities for ice cream and frozen yogurt; and Personnel handles hiring and payroll. How would you organize your folders and files using a file hierarchy of three levels? How would you use folders and subfolders to keep the documents related to these activities distinct and easy to navigate? Draw a diagram and write a short paragraph explaining your answer.
   b. Use tools in the File Explorer window to create the folder hierarchy in the Documents folder on your computer.
   c. Open NotePad and write the path of the Hiring folder, using backslashes to indicate levels in the hierarchy. Do the same for the Testing folder.

2. **Create and save a file.**
   a. Connect your USB flash drive to a USB port on your computer, then open WordPad from the Start menu.
   b. Type **Advertising Campaign** as the title, then start a new line.
   c. Type your name, press [Enter] twice, then create the following list:
   Menu ads
   Email customers
   Web page specials
   Local TV spots
   d. Save the WordPad file with the filename **Advertising Campaign.rtf** in the location where you store your Data Files, view the filename in the WordPad title bar, then close WordPad.

3. **Explore the files and folders on your computer.**
   a. Open a File Explorer window.
   b. Use the Navigation pane to navigate to your USB flash drive or the location where you store your Data Files.
   c. Use the Address bar to navigate to This PC.
   d. Use the File list to navigate to your local hard drive (C:).
   e. Use the File list to open the Users folder, and then open the folder that represents your user name.
   f. Open the Documents folder. (*Hint*: The path is This PC\Local Disk (C:) \Users\Your User Name\Documents.)
   g. Use the Navigation pane to navigate back to This PC.

4. **Change file and folder views.**
   a. Navigate to your Documents folder or the location of your Data Files using the method of your choice.
   b. Use the View tab to view its contents as large icons.
   c. View the folder's contents in the seven other views.
   d. Sort the items in this location by date modified in ascending order.
   e. Open the Preview pane, view a selected item's preview, then close the Preview pane.

5. **Open, edit, and save files.**
   a. Start WordPad, then use the Open dialog box to open the Advertising Campaign.rtf document you created.
   b. After the text "Local TV spots," add a line with the text **Social media**.
   c. Save the document and close WordPad.

6. **Copy files.**
   a. In the File Explorer window, navigate to the location where you store your Data Files if necessary.
   b. Copy the Advertising Campaign.rtf document.
   c. Create a new folder named **Advertising** on your USB flash drive or the location where you store your Data Files (*Hint*: Use the Home tab), then open the folder.
   d. Paste the document copy in the new folder.

7. **Move and rename files.**
   a. Navigate to your USB flash drive or the location where you store your Data Files.
   b. Select the Advertising Campaign.rtf document located there, then cut it.

Skills Review (continued)

    c. Navigate to your Documents folder, then paste the file there.

    d. Rename the file **Advertising Campaign - Backup.rtf**.

8. Search for files and folders.

    a. Use the search box on the taskbar to search for a file using the search text **backup**. (*Hint*: Remember to select My stuff.)

    b. If necessary, scroll to the found file, and notice its path.

    c. Open the Advertising Campaign - Backup document from the search results, then close WordPad. (*Hint*: Closing the program automatically closes any open documents.)

    d. Open a File Explorer window, click in the search box, search your USB flash drive using the search text **overview**.

    e. Open the found document from the File list, then close WordPad.

9. Delete and restore files.

    a. Navigate to your Documents folder.

    b. Verify that your Delete preference is Show recycle confirmation, then delete the Advertising Campaign - Backup.rtf file.

    c. Open the Recycle Bin, and restore the document to its original location.

    d. Navigate to your Documents folder, then move the Advertising Campaign - Backup.rtf file to the Advertising folder on your USB flash drive (or the location where you store your Data Files).

Independent Challenge 1

To meet the needs of gardeners in your town, you have opened a vacation garden care business named GreenerInc. Customers hire you to care for their gardens when they go on vacation. To promote your new business, your website designer asks you to give her selling points to include in a web ad.

    a. Connect your USB flash drive to your computer, if necessary.

    b. Create a new folder named **GreenerInc** on your USB flash drive or the location where you store your Data Files.

    c. In the GreenerInc folder, create two subfolders named **Handouts** and **Website**.

    d. Use WordPad to create a short paragraph or list that describes three advantages of your business. Use **GreenerInc Selling Points** as the first line, followed by the paragraph or list. Include your name and email address after the text.

    e. Save the WordPad document with the filename **Selling Points.rtf** in the Website folder, then close the document and exit WordPad.

    f. Open a File Explorer window, then navigate to the Website folder.

    g. View the contents in at least three different views, then choose the view option that you prefer.

    h. Copy the Selling Points.rtf file, then paste a copy in the Documents folder.

    i. Rename the copied file **Selling Points Backup.rtf**.

    j. Cut the Selling Points Backup.rtf file from the Documents folder, and paste it in the GreenerInc\Website folder in the location where you store your Data Files, then close the File Explorer window.

Independent Challenge 2

As a freelance webpage designer for nonprofit businesses, you depend on your computer to meet critical deadlines. Whenever you encounter a computer problem, you contact a computer consultant who helps you resolve the problem. This consultant has asked you to document, or keep records of, your computer's available drives.

    a. Connect your USB flash drive to your computer, if necessary.

    b. Open File Explorer and go to This PC so you can view information on your drives and other installed hardware.

    c. View the window contents using three different views, then choose the one you prefer.

    d. Open WordPad and create a document with the text **My Drives** and your name on separate lines. Save the document as **My Drives.rtf**.

Independent Challenge 2 (continued)

e. Use Snap Assist to view the WordPad and File Explorer windows next to each other on the screen. (*Hint*: Drag the title bar of one of the windows to the left side of the screen.)

f. In WordPad, list the names of the hard drive (or drives), devices with removable storage, and any other hardware devices installed on the computer as shown in the Devices and Drives section of the window.

g. Switch to a view that displays the total size and amount of free space on your hard drive(s) and removable storage drive(s), and edit each WordPad list item to include the amount of free space for each one (for example, 22.1 GB free of 95.5 GB).

h. Save the WordPad document with the filename **My Drives** on your USB flash drive or the location where you store your Data Files.

i. Close WordPad, then maximize the File Explorer window. Navigate to your file storage location, then preview your document in the Preview pane, and close the window.

Independent Challenge 3

You are an attorney at Garcia and Chu, a large accounting firm. You participate in the company's community outreach program by speaking at career days in area schools. You teach students about career opportunities available in the field of accounting. You want to create a folder structure to store the files for each session.

a. Connect your USB flash drive to your computer (if necessary), then open the window for your USB flash drive or the location where you store your Data Files.

b. Create a folder named **Career Days**.

c. In the Career Days folder, create a subfolder named **Valley Intermediate**. Open this folder, then close it.

d. Use WordPad to create a document with the title **Accounting Jobs** at the top of the page and your name on separate lines, and the following list of items:
Current Opportunities:
Bookkeeper
Accounting Clerk
Accountant
Certified Public Accountant (CPA)

e. Save the WordPad document with the filename **Accounting Jobs.rtf** in the Valley Intermediate folder. (*Hint*: After you switch to your USB flash drive in the Save As dialog box, open the Career Days folder, then open the Valley Intermediate folder before saving the file.) Close WordPad.

f. Open WordPad and the Accounting Jobs document again, add **Senior Accountant** after Accountant, then save the file and close WordPad.

g. Store a copy of the file using the Save As command to your Documents folder, renaming it **Accounting Jobs - Copy.rtf**, then close WordPad.

h. In File Explorer, delete the document copy in your Documents folder so it is placed in the Recycle Bin, then restore it.

i. Open the Recycle Bin window, snap the File Explorer to the left side of the screen and the Recycle in to the right side, then verify that the file has been restored to the correct location.

j. Cut the file from the Documents folder and paste it in the Career Days\Valley Intermediate folder in your Data File storage location, then close all windows.

Independent Challenge 4: Explore

Think of a hobby or volunteer activity that you do now, or one that you would like to start. You will use your computer to help you manage your plans or ideas for this activity.

a. Using paper and pencil, sketch a folder structure with at least two subfolders to contain your documents for this activity.

b. Connect your USB flash drive to your computer, then open the window for your USB flash drive.

Independent Challenge 4: Explore (continued)

c. In File Explorer, create the folder structure for your activity, using your sketch as a reference.

d. Think of at least three tasks that you can do to further your work in your chosen activity.

e. Start a new WordPad document. Add the title **Next Steps** at the top of the page and your name on the next line.

f. Below your name, list the three tasks. Save the file in one of the folders created on your USB flash drive, with the title **To Do.rtf**.

g. Close WordPad, then open a File Explorer window and navigate to the folder where you stored the document.

h. Create a copy of the file, place the copied file in your Documents folder, then rename this file with a name you choose.

i. Delete the copied file from your Documents folder, restore it, then cut and paste the file into the folder that contains your To Do.rtf file, ensuring that the filename of the copy is different so it doesn't overwirte the To Do.rtf file.

j. Open Microsoft Edge using its button on the taskbar, click in the search text box, then search for information about others doing your desired hobby or volunteer activity.

k. Click the Make a Web Note button ![icon] at the top of the window, click the Highlighter tool, then highlight an item that interests you.

l. Click the Share button ![icon], click Mail, choose your desired email account, then send the annotated page to yourself. You will receive an email with an attachment showing the annotated page.

m. Close Edge, your email program, and any open windows.

Visual Workshop

Create the folder structure shown in **FIGURE 2-28** on your USB flash drive (or in the location where you store your Data Files). Create a WordPad document containing your name and today's date, type the path to the Midsize folder, and save it with the filename **Midsize.rtf** in a Midsize folder on your USB Flash drive or the location where you store your Data Files.

FIGURE 2-28

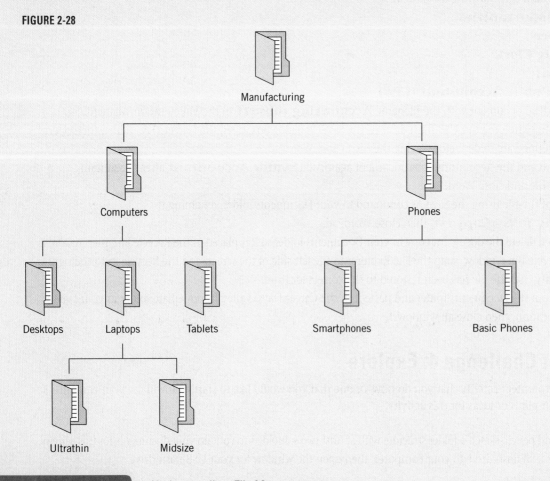

Understanding File Management

Glossary

Accessories Simple Windows application programs (apps) that perform specific tasks, such as the Calculator accessory for performing calculations. Also called Windows accessories.

Action Center Opened by clicking the Notifications button on the right side of the taskbar; shows notifications, tips, and reminders. Contains Quick Actions buttons for commonly-used Windows settings.

Active window The window you are currently using; if multiple windows are open, the window in front of other open windows.

Address A sequence of drive and folder names that describes a folder's or file's location in the file hierarchy; the highest hierarchy level is on the left, with lower hierarchy levels separated by the ▶ symbol to its right.

Address bar In a window, the area just below the Ribbon that shows the file hierarchy, or address of the files that appear in the file list below it; the address appears as a series of links you can click to navigate to other locations on your computer.

App An application program; Windows 10 apps are smaller apps available at the Windows store. Desktop apps, such as Microsoft Office, are more full-featured programs and are available from many software companies.

App window The window that opens after you start an app, showing you the tools you need to use the program and any open program documents.

Application program Any program that lets you work with files or create and edit files such as graphics, letters, financial summaries, and other useful documents, as well as view Web pages on the Internet and send and receive e-mail. Also called an app.

Backup A duplicate copy of a file that is stored in another location.

Border A window's edge; you can drag to resize the window.

Button A small rectangle you can click in order to issue a command to an application program.

Canvas In the Paint accessory, the area in the center of the app window that you use to create drawings.

Case sensitive An application program's (app's) ability to differentiate between uppercase and lowercase letters; usually used to describe how an operating system evaluates passwords that users type to gain entry to user accounts.

Check box A box that turns an option on when checked or off when unchecked.

Click To quickly press and release the left button on the pointing device; also called single-click. The touch-screen equivalent is a tap on the screen.

Clipboard A location in a computer's random access memory that stores information you copy or cut.

Close button In a Windows title bar, the rightmost button; closes the open window, app, and/or document.

Cloud storage location File storage locations on the World Wide Web, such as Windows OneDrive or Dropbox.

Command An instruction to perform a task, such as opening a file or emptying the Recycle Bin.

Copy To make a duplicate copy of a file, folder, or other object that you want to store in another location.

Cortana The digital personal assistant that comes with Windows 10 and Windows phones; can search, give you reminders, alarms, directions, news, weather, and more.

Default In an app window or dialog box, a value that is automatically set; you can change the default to any valid value.

Desktop apps Application programs (apps), such as Microsoft Word, that are full-featured and that are often purchased, either from the Windows Store or from a software developer; also called traditional apps.

Device A hardware component that is part of your computer system, such as a disk drive, a pointing device, or a touch screen device.

Dialog box A window with controls that lets you tell Windows how you want to complete an application program's (app's) command.

Documents folder The folder on your hard drive used to store most of the files you create or receive from others; might contain subfolders to organize the files into smaller groups.

Document window The portion of a application program's (app's) window in which you create the document; displays all or part of an open document.

Double-click To quickly press and release or click the left button on the pointing device twice. The touch-screen equivalent is a double-tap on the screen.

Drag To point to an object, press and hold the left button on the pointing device, move the object to a new location, and then release the left button. Touch-screen users can press and hold a location, then move along the screen with a finger or stylus.

Drag and drop To use a pointing device to move or copy a file or folder directly to a new location instead of using the Clipboard.

Drive A physical location on your computer where you can store files.

Drive name A name for a drive that consists of a letter followed by a colon, such as C: for the hard disk drive.

Dropbox A free online storage site that lets you transfer files that can be retrieved by other people you invite. *See also* Cloud storage location.

Edit To make changes to a file.

File A collection of information stored on your computer, such as a letter, video, or app.

File Explorer A Windows app that allows you to navigate your computer's file hierarchy and manage your files and folders.

File extension A three- or four-letter sequence, preceded by a period, at the end of a filename that identifies the file as a particular type of document; for example, documents in the Rich Text Format have the file extension .rtf.

File hierarchy The tree-like structure of folders and files on your computer.

File list A section of a window that shows the contents of the folder or drive currently selected in the Navigation pane.

File management The ability to organize folders and files on your computer.

File syncing Changes to files stored in the Cloud are automatically synced to all devices.

Filename A unique, descriptive name for a file that identifies the file's content.

Filter To show only a selected group of files; click the arrow icon to the right of a field name in a File Explorer window.

Folder An electronic container that helps you organize your computer files, like a cardboard folder on your desk; it can contain subfolders for organizing files into smaller groups.

Folder name A unique, descriptive name for a folder that helps identify the folder's contents.

Gesture An action you take with your fingertip directly on a touch screen, such as tapping or swiping, to make a selection or perform a task.

Group In a Microsoft app window's Ribbon, a section containing related command buttons.

Hard disk A built-in, high-capacity, high-speed storage medium for all the software, folders, and files on a computer. Also called a hard drive.

Highlighted Describes the changed appearance of an item or other object, usually a change in its color, background color, and/or border; often used for an object on which you will perform an action, such as a desktop icon.

Icon A small image that represents an item, such as the Recycle Bin on your Windows desktop; you can rearrange, add, and delete desktop icons.

Inactive window An open window you are not currently using; if multiple windows are open, the window(s) behind the active window.

Insertion point In a document or filename, a blinking, vertical bar that indicates where the next character you type will appear.

Keyword A descriptive word or phrase you enter to obtain a list of results that include that word or phrase.

Layout An arrangement of files or folders in a window, such as Large icons or Details. There are eight layouts available.

Link Text or an image that you click to display another location, such as a Help topic, a Web site, or a device.

List box A box that displays a list of options from which you can choose (you may need to scroll and adjust your view to see additional options in the list).

Live tile Updated, "live" content that appears on some apps' tiles on the Windows Start menu, including the Weather app and the News app.

Lock screen The screen that appears when you first start your computer, or after you leave it unattended for a period of time, before the sign-in screen.

Log in To select a user account name when a computer starts up, giving access to that user's files. Also called sign in.

Maximize button On the right side of a window's title bar, the center button of three buttons; used to expand a window so that it fills the entire screen. In a maximized window, this button changes to a Restore button.

Maximized window A window that fills the desktop.

Menu A list of related commands.

Microsoft account A web service that lets users sign on to one web address so they can use Windows 10 computers as well as Outlook.com.

Microsoft Edge New in Windows 10, the Microsoft Web browser that is intended to replace Internet Explorer.

Microsoft OneDrive A Microsoft Web site where you can obtain free file storage space, using your own account, that you can share with others; you can access OneDrive from a laptop, tablet computer, or smartphone.

Microsoft Store A website, accessible from the Store icon in the Windows 10 taskbar, where you can purchase and download apps, including games, productivity tools, and media software.

Microsoft Windows 10 An operating system.

Minimize button On the right side of a window's title bar, the leftmost button of three buttons; use to reduce a window so that it only appears as an icon on the taskbar.

Minimized window A window that is visible only as an icon on the taskbar.

Mouse pointer A small arrow or other symbol on the screen that you move by manipulating the pointing device; also called a pointer.

Move To change the location of a file, folder, or other object by physically placing it in another location.

Navigate down To move to a lower level in your computer's file hierarchy.

Navigate up To move to a higher level in your computer's file hierarchy.

Navigation pane The left pane in a window that contains links to folders and device locations; click an item in the Navigation pane to display its contents in the file list or click the ⌄ or ⟩ symbols to display or hide subfolders in the Navigation pane.

Notification area An area on the right side of the Windows 10 taskbar that displays the current time as well as icons representing selected information; the Notifications button displays pop-up messages when a program on your computer needs your attention. Click the Notifications button to display the Action Center. *See also* Action Center.

Operating system A program that manages the complete operation of your computer and lets you interact with it.

Option button A small circle in a dialog box that you click to select only one of two or more related options.

Pane A section of a window, such as the Navigation pane in the File Explorer window.

Password A special sequence of numbers and letters that users can employ to control who can access the files in their user account area; keeping the password private helps keep users' computer information secure.

Paste To place a copied item from the Clipboard to a location in a document.

Path An address that describes the exact location of a file in a file hierarchy; shows the folder with the highest hierarchy level on the left and steps through each hierarchy level toward the right. Locations are separated by small triangles or by backslashes.

Photos app A Windows 10 app that lets you view and organize your pictures.

Point To position the tip of the mouse pointer over an object, option, or item.

Pointer *See* Mouse pointer.

Pointing device A device that lets you interact with your computer by controlling the movement of the mouse pointer on your computer screen; examples include a mouse, trackball, touchpad, pointing stick, on-screen touch pointer, or a tablet.

Pointing device action A movement you execute with your computer's pointing device to communicate with the computer; the five basic pointing device actions are point, click, double-click, drag, and right-click.

Power button The physical button on your computer that turns your computer on.

Preview pane A pane on the right side of a File Explorer window that shows the actual contents of a selected file without opening an app; might not work for some types of files, such as databases.

Program A set of instructions written for a computer, such as an operating system program or an application program; also called an application or an app.

Quick Access buttons Buttons that appear at the bottom of the Windows Action Center; single-click to perform common actions such as turning WiFi on or off.

Quick Access toolbar A small toolbar on the left side of a Microsoft application program window's title bar, containing icons that you click to quickly perform common actions, such as saving a file.

Quick Access view A list of frequently-used folders and recently used files that appears when you first open File Explorer.

RAM (Random Access Memory) The storage location that is part of every computer, that temporarily stores open apps and document data while a computer is on.

Recycle Bin A desktop object that stores folders and files you delete from your hard drive(s) and enables you to restore them.

Removable storage Storage media that you can easily transfer from one computer to another, such as DVDs, CDs, or USB flash drives.

Restore Down button On the right side of a maximized window's title bar, the center of three buttons; use to reduce a window to its last non-maximized size. In a restored window, this button changes to a Maximize button.

Ribbon In many Microsoft app windows, a horizontal strip near the top of the window that contains tabs (pages) of grouped command buttons that you click to interact with the app.

Rich Text Format (RTF) The file format that the WordPad app uses to save files.

Right-click To press and release the right button on the pointing device; use to display a shortcut menu with commands you issue by left-clicking them.

RTF *See* Rich Text Format.

ScreenTip A small box containing informative text that appears when you position the mouse over an object; identifies the object when you point to it.

Scroll To adjust your view to see portions of the app window that are not currently in a window.

Scroll arrow A button at each end of a scroll bar for adjusting your view in a window in small increments in that direction.

Scroll bar A vertical or horizontal bar that appears along the right or bottom side of a window when there is more content than can be displayed within the window, so that you can adjust your view.

Scroll box A box in a scroll bar that you can drag to display a different part of a window.

Search criteria Descriptive text that helps identify the application program (app), folder, file, or Web site you want to locate when conducting a search.

Search Tools tab A tab that appears in the File Explorer window after you click the Search text box; lets you specify a specific search location, limit your search, repeat previous searches, save searches, and open a folder containing a found file.

Select To change the appearance of an item by clicking, double-clicking, or dragging across it, to indicate that you want to perform an action on it.

Select pointer The mouse pointer shape that looks like a white arrow pointing toward the upper-left corner of the screen.

Shortcut An icon that acts as a link to an app, file, folder, or device that you use frequently.

Shortcut menu A menu of context-appropriate commands for an object that opens when you right-click that object.

Shut down To exit the operating system and turn off your computer.

Sign in To select a user account name when a computer starts up, giving access to that user's files. Also called log in.

Single-click See Click.

Snap assist feature The Windows 10 feature that lets you drag a window to the left or right side of the screen, where it "snaps" to fill that half of the screen and displays remaining open windows as thumbnails you click to fill the other half.

Sort Change the order of, such as the order of files or folders in a window, based on criteria such as date, file size, or alphabetical by filename.

Spin box A text box with up and down arrows; you can type a setting in the text box or click the arrows to increase or decrease the setting.

Start button A clickable button at in the lower left corner of the Windows 10 screen that you click to open the Start menu.

Start menu Appears after you click the Start button; provides access to all programs, documents, and settings on the computer.

Subfolder A folder within another folder.

Tab A page in an application program's Ribbon, or in a dialog box, that contains a group of related commands and settings.

Task view A new Windows 10 area, accessible from the Task view button on the taskbar, that lets you switch applications and create multiple desktops (also called virtual desktops).

Taskbar The horizontal bar at the bottom of the Windows 10 desktop; displays icons representing apps, folders, and/or files on the left, and the Notification area, containing the date and time and special program messages, on the right.

Text box An area in a Windows program that you click to enter text.

Tile A shaded rectangle on the Windows 10 Start menu that represents an app. See also App and Application program.

Title bar The shaded top border of a window that displays the name of the window, folder, or file and the app name. Darker shading indicates the active window.

Toolbar In an application program, a set of buttons, lists, and menus you can use to issue program commands.

Universal apps See Windows 10 apps.

USB flash drive A removable storage device for folders and files that you plug into a USB port on your computer; makes it easy to transport folders and files to other computers. Also called a pen drive, flash drive, jump drive, keychain drive, or thumb drive.

User account A special area in a computer's operating system where users can store their own files and preferences.

User interface The controls that let you interact with an operating system or an application program (app).

View A set of appearance choices for folder contents, such as Large Icons view or Details view.

Window A rectangular-shaped work area that displays an app or a collection of files, folders, and Windows tools.

Window control buttons The set of three buttons on the right side of a window's title bar that let you control the window's state, such as minimized, maximized, restored to its previous open size, or closed.

Windows Action Center A pane that appears in the lower right corner of the Windows 10 screen that lets you quickly view system notifications and selected settings; also has Quick Action buttons to perform common actions in one click.

Windows app Small program available for free or for purchase in the Windows Store; can run on Windows desktops, laptops, tablets, and phones.

Windows 10 apps Apps (application programs) for Windows 10 that often have a single purpose, such as Photos, News, or OneDrive.

Windows 10 UI The Windows 10 user interface. See also User interface.

Windows accessories Application programs (apps), such as Paint or WordPad, that come with the Windows 10 operating system.

Windows 10 desktop An electronic work area that lets you organize and manage your information, much like your own physical desktop.

Windows Search The Windows feature that lets you look for files and folders on your computer storage devices; to search, type text in the Search text box in the title bar of any open window, or click the Start button and type text in the search text box.

Index